J. C. Mapstone

June 1974

ACTION, EMOTION AND WILL

STUDIES IN
PHILOSOPHICAL PSYCHOLOGY

Edited by
R. F. HOLLAND

Mental Acts	P. T. Geach
The Psychology of Perception	D. W. Hamlyn
The Unconscious	Alasdair MacIntyre
The Concept of Motivation	R. S. Peters
The Idea of a Social Science	Peter Winch
Dreaming	Norman Malcolm
Free Action	A. I. Melden
Bodily Sensations	D. M. Armstrong
Sensationalism and Scientific Explanation	Peter Alexander
Action, Emotion and Will	Anthony Kenny
Rationality	Johnathan Bennett

ACTION, EMOTION AND WILL

by

ANTHONY KENNY

LONDON
ROUTLEDGE & KEGAN PAUL
NEW YORK: HUMANITIES PRESS

First published 1963
by Routledge & Kegan Paul Limited
Broadway House, 68–74 Carter Lane
London, E.C.4

Second impression 1964
Third impression 1966
Fourth impression 1969

Printed in Great Britain
by Lowe & Brydone (Printers) Limited
London

SBN 7100 3839 9

CONTENTS

PREFACE

SEVERAL of the chapters of this book were
read in draft to seminars and philosophical
societies in various parts of England. I am grateful
to those who took part in the discussion at such
meetings for many helpful criticisms. I am particularly indebted to Mr Anthony Quinton, Miss
Elizabeth Anscombe, Mr Peter Geach, and
Professor A. N. Prior for their kind encouragement and for numerous valuable suggestions. I
must thank also Mr David Pears, Mr Patrick
Gardiner, and Mr Roy Holland for pointing out
several mistakes which I have tried to correct. I
must also record my gratitude for having been
allowed to consult some unpublished notes of
Wittgenstein's which were of great assistance in
the writing of Chapter Three.

A. K.

CHAPTER ONE

THE PASSIONS OF THE SOUL

THE concepts employed in the description, explanation, and appraisal of human conduct have been regarded since antiquity as subjects of philosophical interest. From the Renaissance, however, until quite recent times, the major interest of philosophers has been epistemology. Research has been centred on the contemplative rather than the active, on the intellectual rather than the emotional and voluntary aspects of human life. Knowledge rather than action, belief rather than emotion, the intellect rather than the will have been the central topics of philosophical concern. Moral philosophy has indeed been written in abundance: but it has not, for the most part, been based on any systematic examination of the concepts involved in the description and explanation of those human actions which it is the function of morals to enjoin or forbid, to criticise and to appraise.

The major philosophers of the seventeenth and eighteenth centuries did not indeed altogether neglect the study of the emotions and the will. Descartes wrote his pamphlet *Les Passions de l'Ame*, while Hume interposed in his *Treatise*, between the book on the understanding and that entitled "Of Morals" a third book treating expressly "Of the Passions". But these books have remained among the least discussed, as they are among the least successful, of their output.

I shall begin the first part of this book with a consideration of the account which these philosophers gave of the emotions. Having attempted to show how their theories were vitiated by a mistaken epistemological approach, I shall discuss the influence which they had on the experimental examination of the emotions. I shall then treat separately some of the problems which are raised by a consideration of the emotions and pass finally to the allied topics of desire and pleasure.

Descartes, in his treatise on *The Passions of the Soul*, deals with fear, anger, joy, love, admiration, respect, scorn, pride, humility, bravery, pity, sadness, "and other similar sentiments". The passions of the soul are a sub-class of "the things which we experience in ourselves". There are some things, such as heat and movement, which we experience in ourselves, but which can also exist in inanimate bodies: these are to be attributed not to the soul, but to the body. To our soul we must attribute only those of the objects of our experience which are "*pensées*". Not all *pensées*, however, are *passions* of the soul: some are "*volontés*" which originate in the soul alone, and therefore deserve rather to be called actions. Those *pensées* in which the soul is passive are perceptions, and these again are of two kinds: those which are caused by the soul, and those which are caused by the body, that is to say, by the action of the animal spirits on the soul.

2

An example of the former class is the perception of our *volontés*: "for it is certain that we cannot will anything without perceiving *ipso facto* that we will it". The latter class is divided finally into three sub-classes: there are some perceptions which we refer to outside objects, others to our bodies, and others to our soul. It is this last class which alone rightly deserves the name "passions of the soul". "The perceptions which are referred only to the soul are those whose effects are felt as if in the soul itself, and of which normally no proximate cause is known to which they can be attributed. Such are the sentiments of joy, anger, and others like them".

The peculiar characteristic of these perceptions which are called "the passions of the soul" is the infallibility which we enjoy in their regard. We may be deceived by perceptions referred to external bodies, and by perceptions referred to our own, such as feelings of hunger and pain. But we cannot be deceived in the same way by our passions. "They are so close and so interior to our soul that it is impossible that they should be felt without their being in reality just as they are felt." "Even if a man is asleep and dreaming, it is impossible that he should feel sad, or feel moved by any other passion, without it being strictly true that such a passion is in the soul" (*Les Passions de l'Ame*, 17–26).

Having thus delimited the class of passions, Descartes defines them as follows. The passions of the soul are "perceptions, sentiments or emotions of the soul, which are referred particularly to the soul itself, and which are caused, continued, and strengthened by some movement of the animal spirits". His reason for calling them "sentiments" or "feelings" is interesting: "they are received into the soul in the same fashion as the objects of the exterior senses, and are known by it in exactly the same manner" (*Op. cit.*, 28).

In Descartes' exposition of his theory so far there appears a certain obscurity. How can he say both that the passions of the soul are among the perceptions which are caused by the body, while defining them as those "*desquelles on ne connoist communément aucune cause prochaine, à laquelle on les puisse rapporter*"? And what does he mean by saying that they are "*les perceptions . . . dont on sent les effets comme en l'âme mesme*" (*Op. cit.*, 25)? And how can he say that indubitability is a peculiar characteristic of the passions, since he elsewhere attributes it to all our sensations strictly so called (*Philosophical Writings*, 71)?

His remarks become intelligible only in the light of his own theory of perception. "When we say we perceive colours in objects," he wrote in *Principles of Philosophy*, "it is really just the same as though we said that we perceived in objects something as to whose nature we are ignorant, but which produces in us a very manifest and obvious sensation, called the sensation of colour" (*Op. cit.*, 195). When, therefore, we say that we see a red apple, we are, on Descartes' view, attributing our sensation of redness to the apple as a cause. Again, when we say that we feel pain in the foot, we are, according to Descartes, recording a sensation in the mind and attributing it to a disturbance in the foot as a cause. So that when Descartes says that for the passions, unlike sensations which we refer to our own or other bodies, no proximate cause is commonly known to which they can be attributed, he is referring to the fact that when we feel a passion such as fear, we do not attribute the fear to any external object as we attribute the redness to the apple, nor do we locate it in any part of our body as we locate pain in our foot. It is well known that, for Descartes, the causal hypotheses embodied in ordinary-language reports of perception or sensation could be mistaken, though reports of the pure mental events of perception and sensation, pure *cogitationes*, were immune from error. It is because reports of the passions report purely a mental event, and embody no hypotheses about the cause of this event, that they enjoy the peculiar infallibility which Descartes ascribes to them. The perceptions which are referred to our own or other bodies may deceive us, since they may tempt us to frame incorrect hypotheses; the perceptions which are the passions cannot so deceive us, since they tempt us to frame no hypotheses at all (*Op. cit.*, 71, 122–123).

Though reports of the passions do not ascribe them to any physical cause, yet, Descartes insists, the passions have physical causes. The immediate cause of a passion, as of any perception or sensation, is a motion of the pineal gland brought about by animal spirits. But the passions are not felt in the pineal gland any more than colour is seen, or pain is felt, in the pineal gland. They are felt, says Descartes, in the soul itself: "*les perceptions qu'on rapporte seulement a l'âme sont celles dont on sent les effets comme en l'âme mesme*".

Again, though the passions have no proximate physical cause in the way in which sensations of

5

colour have a proximate physical cause, they do most commonly have remote physical causes. That is to say, the motion of the pineal gland which is the immediate cause of the passion, itself has a cause. This cause may be a fortuitous disturbance in the brain, or some other part of the body, "as happens when one feels sad or joyful without being able to assign any object of one's sadness or joy". But commonly the cause of the motion of the animal spirits is some object which acts upon our senses.

Why does Descartes list the passions among the perceptions which are caused by the body? Since they are not "referred to the body", it might have seemed more appropriate to class them among the perceptions which are caused by the soul alone. This is the one step in his classification which he does not here justify: but the reason is in fact obvious to anyone familiar with his general position. It is that the passions —as he remarks later—are not subject to voluntary control. In the sixth Meditation Descartes gives the fact that sensations are not subject to voluntary control as the best reason for believing that they proceed from bodies distinct from consciousness. "I certainly had some reason," he writes, "to think that I was aware in sensation of objects quite different from my own consciousness: viz. bodies from which the ideas proceeded. For it was my experience that the ideas came to me without any consent of mine; so that I could neither have a sensation of any object, however I wished, if it was not present to the sense-organ, nor help having the sensation when that object was present" (*Op. cit.*, 112).

It would take us too far round to follow Descartes'

inquiry into the nature of the several passions. But there are several points of general interest which emerge. It is clear that he conceives his main task to be to frame hypotheses concerning the mechanisms by which external objects give rise to passions in the soul: the passions are differentiated from each other partly by the different external objects which cause them, and partly by the differing mechanisms by which they are brought into being. Fear, for example, is explained in the following manner. An approaching animal prints an image of itself on each of our eyes; in the pineal gland these two images are fused into a single image which acts immediately on the soul, thus making it see the animal. If the animal is of a frightening kind, the sight of it arouses various passions in the soul: that is to say, the animal spirits which make up the image scatter, some of them travel to the heart and some of them travel to the nerves which serve to turn the back and to move the legs in flight. The movement of the spirits to the heart gives an impulse to the pineal gland, which causes fear in the soul; the movement to the flight nerves gives the gland a different impulse, which causes the perception of the flight. Thus flight may be caused by a purely corporeal process, without any intervention of the soul; and similarly, joy may make one swoon by opening the orifices of the heart so widely that the blood floods in and puts out the fire in the heart before it can be rarefied and expelled into the veins. But the commonest effect of the passions is to incite the soul to will a course of action for which they merely prepare the body (*Les Passions de l'Ame*, 35–40, 112).

The quaint physiology should not distract us:

Descartes' theory deserves to be treated no less seriously as an essay in philosophy than the James-Lange theory which in some ways it resembles. In its essentials the theory is that the physiological processes involved in the perception of a fearful object set in motion, by purely mechanical causation, a further physiological process which issues in the behaviour characteristic of fear. As, for Descartes, both the perception of the fearful object and the perception of the behaviour manifesting the fear are mental events caused by the physiological processes in question, so the fear itself is a mental event caused by a third physiological process in mechanical causal connection with the first two; or, perhaps more accurately, by another part of one uninterrupted process which constitutes the bodily counterpart of seeing, fearing, and fleeing from a fearful object.

Not only fear, Descartes maintains, but almost all the passions are accompanied by turbulences in the heart and blood and animal spirits. As long as this turbulence lasts, the appropriate passion remains present to our thought, in the same fashion as sensible objects are present to it as long as they are acting upon our sense-organs. For this reason, the passions are only indirectly subject to the control of the will. The *volonté* which is the will not to be angry, say, is not sufficient by itself to prevent one from being angry. The most it can do is to refuse consent to the effects of anger. Anger may make the hand rise in order to strike; the will can ordinarily hold it back from striking (*Op. cit.*, 46).

Voluntary action is, for Descartes, the exact reverse of perception. As perception is an event in the soul

8

caused proximately by a movement in the pineal gland, so voluntary action is an effect caused by a movement in the pineal gland which is itself caused by an event in the soul. Each *volonté* in the soul is linked by nature with a particular motion of the pineal gland; but it is not always the *volonté* to do X which is connected with the movement of the pineal gland which causes X. For instance, the movement of the pineal gland which causes the pupil to contract is not linked with the *volonté* to contract the pupil, but with the *volonté* to see a distant object.

Since the pineal gland may be moved from two different directions, that is to say by a *volonté* from the soul, and by a physiological process of the body, there arises the possibility of tension. It is by means of this that Descartes explains the phenomenon of conflict between the will and the passions. In temptation, for instance, the will to avoid the tempting object pushes the pineal gland one way; while the animal spirits are pushing the gland the other way so as to cause in the soul the desire of the tempting object (*Op. cit.*, 46–47).

Descartes is interested in the teleology of the passions, and is anxious to show how they serve human well-being. He says that they are instituted by nature to incite the soul to consent to and assist such actions as serve to preserve and perfect the body. Nature teaches the soul what objects are beneficial or injurious to the body by means of the sensations of pleasure or pain which accompany the perception of the objects: these sensations produce a train of passions which lead to the action appropriate to conserve the body. Thus the sensation of pain pro-

B   9

duces the passion of sadness, which is followed by the passion of hatred for the painful object, and finally the passion of desire to get rid of it. Or when something is "represented as good for us"—i.e. when accompanied with a sensation of pleasure—it causes love in us which leads to various forms of appropriate voluntary behaviour (*Op. cit.*, 56, 137, 120, 144; *Philosophical Writings*, 117).

Though many passions are thus linked by nature with particular courses of action, not all such links are built in to the human being. Soul and body are so linked, that once a bodily action and an experience have been joined, they always recur together. This explains why not all men have the same passions in the same circumstances; as does the fact that not all men's brains are made alike. Thus if we have a horrible experience while eating a pleasant dish, we may ever after feel repugnance for that dish; a man may have a horror of the smell of roses because early in life he was injured by a rose (*Les Passions de l'Ame*, 39, 50, 136).

Descartes lists five primary passions: gladness and sadness, love and hatred, and desire. The other passions are built up out of these: thus pride is compounded out of gladness and love. This compounding of passions is envisaged as a mechanical combination of the physiological processes which give rise to each of the compounded passions: thus pity, which is a mixture of sadness and love, causes weeping, because love sends blood to the heart, which makes vapours rise to the eyes, while sadness, being a chilling passion, condenses these vapours and expels them in liquid form (*Op. cit.*, 189).

In general, Descartes treats the relation of the

10

object of fear to fear itself as being that of cause to effect. What is feared—say an alarming animal—is the cause of the mental event or entity which is fear. But when he comes to consider such passions as courage ("*hardiesse*"), this pattern is not so easy to apply. One can display courage only in the face of (at least putative) danger. So Descartes says that the object of *hardiesse* is *difficulté*. But it would be odd to say that the danger *causes* courage; normally, says Descartes, it leads to despair, whereas courage involves hope. But instead of distinguishing, as we might expect, between the cause and the object of a passion, Descartes here introduces a distinction between the object and the end of a passion. When the Decii threw themselves beneath their enemies, the object of their bravery was the danger to their lives; the end of their bravery was *pour encourager les autres (Op. cit.*, 173).

Again, in the course of his inquiry into particular passions, Descartes is led to make a distinction between intellectual emotions and passions strictly so called. This distinction is made in the context of a consideration of two features which present a complication in any theory of passions: namely, the hypocritical expression of an emotion which is not felt, and the excitation of emotion in unreal circumstances, as at the theatre, or while reading a book. What happens in such cases, he says, is that there are present at one and the same time a true passion, arising from the body, and also a contrary and stronger intellectual emotion, excited by the soul itself. Thus, if a man weeps for his dead wife, though in fact he would be extremely annoyed if she were to rise from the dead, what happens is that the passion of sadness grips his

11

heart and makes him weep, while in his soul there is a secret joy which is so strong that no passion of sadness can diminish it. Again, if while watching a tragedy we enjoy feeling miserable, what happens is that an intellectual gladness arises from the passion of sadness. These intellectual emotions presumably belong to the class of "perceptions which are caused in the soul by the soul alone", of which Descartes' usual examples are the perception of volitions and images voluntarily entertained. Normally these emotions are joined to the corresponding passions: it is only when they are accompanied by contrary passions that the distinction is brought to our notice (*Op. cit.*, 147).

Leaving aside complications such as have been introduced in the last two paragraphs, we may extract from *Les Passions de l'Ame* three major theses about the emotions.

(1) An emotion is a purely private mental event which is the object of an immediate and infallible spiritual awareness. It is merely contingently connected with its manifestation in behaviour: for one may be certain of its existence while doubting whether one has a body. It is merely contingently connected with its object: for one cannot be mistaken about the existence of a passion, while one may go wrong in assigning it a cause.

(2) There is no difference of category between feelings such as joy, emotions such as love, attitudes such as admiration, virtues such as courage and traits of character such as bashfulness: all alike are passions of the soul. Considered purely as mental events, passions and sensations do not differ from one another except in the way in which one sensation

differs from another. All alike are items of consciousness, objects of the same infallible intuition.

(3) To explain an action as resulting from a passion is to assert that a causal mechanism links the action to the physiological process which produces the passion. It is the task of the philosopher, in giving an account of the passions, to set out the workings of these mechanisms.

Wittgenstein has shown that a purely mental event, such as Descartes conceived an emotion to be, is an *Unding*. Any word purporting to be the name of something observable only by introspection, and merely causally connected with publicly observable phenomena, would have to acquire its meaning by a purely private and uncheckable performance. But no word could acquire a meaning by such a performance; for a word only has meaning as part of a language; and a language is something essentially public and shareable. If the names of the emotions acquire their meaning for each of us by a ceremony from which everyone else is excluded, then none of us can have any idea what anyone else means by the word. Nor can anyone know what he means by the word himself; for to know the meaning of a word is to know how to use it rightly; and where there can be no check on how a man uses a word there is no room to talk of 'right' or 'wrong' use (*Philosophical Investigations, passim*, especially 1, 243–258).

In arguing against the notion of the 'private object' Wittgenstein chose as his example a sensation, pain; no doubt because it is in such cases that it seems most plausible to suggest that a word might acquire a meaning by a private ostensive definition. With the emotions, the Cartesian idea of a purely mental event runs into an extra difficulty. Emotions, unlike pain, have objects: we are afraid *of* things, angry *with* people, ashamed *that* we have done such-and-such. This feature of the emotions, which is sometimes called their 'intensionality', is misrepresented by Descartes, who treats the relation between a passion and its object as a contingent one of effect to cause. Something will be said later about the distinction between the object and the cause of an emotion; and it is well known how difficult it is to give any account on Cartesian principles of a causal relation between physical and spiritual events. Here I will remark merely that the intensionality of the emotions adds a further reason for denying that emotion-words acquire their meanings by some private ostensive definition. Many people are attracted by the idea that the meaning of the word "pain" is learnt by picking out a recurring feature of experience and associating it with the sound of the word. It is much less plausible to suggest that the meaning of "fear" is learnt in the same way, when we reflect how very different from each other fears of different objects may be. *What* is the feature of experience, recognizable by introspection without reference to context, which is common to fear of mice and fear of waking the baby, fear of overpopulation and fear of being overdressed, fear of muddling one's sequence of tenses and fear of hell?

It is now fashionable to renounce Cartesianism; it is not so fashionable to quote Descartes. It is worth doing so, if only because it enables one to show how Cartesian mistakes occur in quite unlikely places.

Descartes' talk of 'the perceptions of the soul', for instance, led him to confuse experiencing an emotion with recognizing an emotion. The same confusion occurs in *The Concept of Mind.* Professor Ryle, in refuting the view that to act out of vanity is to be impelled by feelings of vanity, puts forward the following argument.

To put it quite dogmatically, the vain man never feels vain. . . . There is no special thrill or pang which we call a 'feeling of vanity'. Indeed, if there were such a recognisable specific feeling, and the vain man was constantly experiencing it, he would be the first instead of the last person to recognise how vain he was (p. 87).

This argument appears to rest on a confusion between feeling vain and having vain feelings. To feel vain is to feel that one is vain. It is possible, therefore, to have a vain feeling without feeling vain, in a way in which it is not possible to have a hungry feeling without feeling hungry. A woman, surveying her face in the mirror, may bask cosily in the thought "how beautiful I am!" Such a feeling may well be a feeling of vanity; if, for instance, she is in fact not at all beautiful. But it is not necessary that she should recognise this feeling as a vain feeling; and only if she does will she, then or later, feel vain. Ryle's argument would hold only if Descartes was right in identifying experiencing an emotion with recognizing it.

The Cartesian picture of the emotions has been for so long part of the climate of Western thought that it retains its hold even on those who explicitly reject it, while to those untrained in philosophy it often appears as the natural and commonsense view. It was not always so. Descartes himself was conscious of being an innovator: he began his treatise with the remark that everything the ancients wrote on this topic is worthless. Each of the Cartesian theses listed earlier would have been rejected in the Middle Ages. The idea that the emotions are only contingently connected with their bodily manifestations was foreign to Augustine and Aquinas, both of whom maintained that emotions were inconceivable in a disembodied spirit (*Summa Theologica* Ia, 77, 8). The assimilation of diverse passions to each other and to sensation is in contradiction to the scholastic distinction between *passio* and *habitus* and between appetitive and apprehensive faculties. The denial of the intensionality of the emotions runs counter to the Aristotelian commonplace that the passions are specified by their objects. The medieval physiology was even quainter than the Cartesian; but then the medievals did not regard the philosophy of the emotions as a search for causal mechanisms. For Aquinas, the relation between an emotion and its bodily manifestations was not one of efficient causality. The increase in one's blood pressure when one is angry is, according to him, neither a cause nor an effect of one's anger; it is its *materia* (*In I De Anima*, 1.2.24).

None the less, it was Descartes' formulation of the problems concerning the emotions which was to influence the later history of philosophy and the early attempts to make psychology into an experimental science. He raised, often for the first time, genuine questions which since his day have figured in every discussion of the emotions. The teleological significance of the emotions, lengthily discussed from Darwin to

Sartre; the problem of objectless emotions such as *Angst*, which exercised Freud and Wittgenstein; the counterfeit emotions produced by plays and novels, which provided so many of the data studied by experimental psychologists; all these topics already find a place, though naïvely and unsatisfactorily treated, in *Les Passions de l'Ame*.

When we turn from Descartes to Locke, we find very similar doctrine much less clearly stated. For Locke, pain and pleasure were "simple ideas which we receive both from sensation and reflection", and which accompanied either sensation on the one hand, or the thought or perception of the mind on the other. Like other simple ideas, pain and pleasure "cannot be described, nor their names defined; the way of knowing them is, as of the simple ideas of the senses, only by experience". Though commonly we distinguish between bodily and mental pains and pleasures, Locke thought that "they be only different constitutions of the mind, sometimes occasioned by disorder in the body, sometimes by thoughts of the mind" (*Essay* II, 20).

Pleasure and pain are "the hinges on which our passions turn"; the passions are "the modifications or tempers of the mind ... the internal sensations (if I may so call them) they produce in us." Locke explains in detail how each of a number of passions (love, hatred, desire, joy, sorrow, hope, fear, shame, despair, anger, and envy) are produced by pain and pleasure in different circumstances. Each of the passions is either a delight in the mind, or an uneasiness in the mind, occasioned by some grateful or unacceptable sensation or reflection. Thus, for example, "Hope is that pleasure in the mind, which everyone finds in himself, upon the thought of a probably future enjoyment of a thing which is apt to delight him". "The passions," he notes, "have most of them, in most persons, operations on the body, and cause various changes in it; which not being always sensible, do not make a necessary part of the idea of each passion." Shame, for example, may or may not be accompanied by blushing.

The general pattern of the accounts which Locke gives of the several passions is as follows. A passion is either a delight (as in joy and hope) or an uneasiness (as in fear and shame) of the mind, consequent upon certain thoughts, such as the thought of a future pleasure or a past pain.[1] Love and hatred, on the other hand, are described not as pains and pleasures in themselves, but rather as the thought of pain and pleasure. Thus hatred is "the thought of the pain which anything present or absent is apt to produce in us".[2] On the other hand, the argument Locke gives in

[1] "Delight" and "uneasiness" are for Locke just other names for pleasure and pain.

[2] What Locke actually says is that love is the thought of the thought of a pleasure. "Any one reflecting upon the thought he has of the delight which any present or absent thing is apt to produce in him, has the idea we call *love*." (*loc. cit.*). But he cannot mean anything quite so implausible, since he gives a different account of hatred (quoted above) which is clearly meant to correspond. The confusion is caused by the constant ambiguity of Locke's use of the word "idea". "To have an idea of S" for Locke may mean *inter alia* (a) "to experience S" (b) "to know what the word "S" means" (c) "to give a philosophical account of S". Each of these senses occurs in the context in question. The confusion is both the ground and the result of Locke's view that one learns what a word means by experiencing what it stands for and that it is impossible to give a philosophical account of a word standing for an experience other

18

support of his definition of love[1] suggests that he wanted to say that love and hatred were the pain and pleasure themselves, and not merely the thought of these. This would bring his account of love and hatred into line with his account of the other passions. But the whole discussion is confused. He will speak at one moment of the passions as being pains and pleasures, at another of their being caused by pains and pleasures, and at another of their terminating in pain and pleasure.

In an earlier passage, he gives a different account, in which the passions appear not as ideas, but as operations of the mind upon ideas, by reflection on which, that is to say through the agency of the internal sense, the ideas *of* these passions are formed. Thus he writes that ideas are furnished to the understanding "by the perception of the operations of our own mind within us . . . The term *operations* here I use in a large sense as comprehending not barely the actions of the mind about its ideas, but some sort of passions arising sometimes from them, such as is the satisfaction or uneasiness from any thought." (*Op. cit.* II, 1). The mind observes its operations by means of the internal sense, and thus acquires the ideas of these operations.

We are thus left in doubt whether a passion such as

than by exhorting the reader to introspect. It seems probable, there-fore, that what Locke meant was "Anyone reflecting upon the thought . . . has the idea *of* what we call love". But it is quite likely that he did not know *what* he meant; and that he thought "love" and "the idea of love" were interchangeable as "Berlin" and "the city of Berlin" are.

[1] "When a man declares . . . that he loves grapes, it is no more but that the taste of grapes delights him."

THE PASSIONS OF THE SOUL

anger is an operation of the mind about an idea (e.g. the idea of an insult) or the perception of this operation by the internal sense. This confusion is impossible to resolve, since "the idea of anger" may mean *either* that internal phenomenon which we call "anger", *or* the thought of anger.

The notion of anger as an internal phenomenon, and the comparison between feeling anger and, say, feeling solidity, on which Locke's account is based, are both mistaken. But Locke's discussion is so incoherent, even on his own premisses, that it would be waste of time to discuss it in detail. The empiricist view of the emotions finds a more plausible exponent in Hume. Some at least of the ambiguities of Locke's 'ideas' are clarified by Hume's distinction between 'impressions' ("our sensations, passions, and emotions, as they make their first appearance in the soul") and 'ideas' ("the faint images of these in thinking and reasoning"). When Hume talks of "having an idea of love" we will not be in doubt, as we were with Locke, whether he means "being in love" or "thinking about love".

For Hume, as for Descartes, a passion is a particular sort of experience. "As all the perceptions of the mind may be divided into *impressions* and *ideas*, so the impressions admit of another division into *original* and *secondary*" (*Treatise* II, 1, 1). Original impressions include the impressions of the senses and all bodily pains and pleasures: they "strike upon the senses" and "make us perceive heat or cold, thirst or hunger, pleasure or pain, of some kind or other" (*Op. cit.* I, 1, 2). Secondary impressions, or impressions of reflection, are "such as proceed from some of these original

THE PASSIONS OF THE SOUL

ones, either immediately or by the interposition of its idea" (*Op. cit.* II, 1, 1). These secondary impressions are the passions: and these in their turn may be divided into calm passions (such as aesthetic emotions) and violent passions (passions strictly so called, such as love). The way in which secondary impressions are distinguished from, and related to, the primary impressions is illustrated as follows: "A fit of the gout produces a long train of passions, as grief, hope, fear; but is not derived immediately from any affection or idea" (*ibid*).

The relation between a passion and the person, or perhaps rather the mind, to which it belongs is conceived by Hume as the relation of perceived to perceiver. "Nothing," he writes, "is ever present with the mind but its perceptions or impressions and ideas. . . . To hate, to love, to think, to feel, to see; all this is nothing but to perceive" (*Op. cit.* I, 2, 6). Since seeing a woman is one way of perceiving a woman, it might appear from this passage that Hume thought that loving a woman was another way of perceiving her. But no: what is perceived when a passion is felt is the passion itself. Hume does not talk as rashly as Locke of an 'internal sense'; but in numerous passages he makes it clear that he thinks along similar lines. He warns us, for instance, that "the passions may decay into so soft an emotion, as to become, in a manner imperceptible" (II, 1, 1). By "imperceptible" he means "imperceptible to the person who has the passion", not "imperceptible to others". This is clear from another passage where he explains how the vulgar believe that they are motivated by reason when they are in fact influenced by the calm passions.

The calm passions (such as kindness to children) "produce little emotion in the mind, and are more known by their effects than by the immediate feeling or sensation." Since reason also produces no emotion, the calm passions are "confounded with reason by all those who judge of things from the first view and appearance" (*Op. cit.* II, 3, 3). Again, two passions may be so alike that the difference between them is imperceptible to the mind to which they belong; and indeed if a large number of passions are present to the mind at the same time, it may not be able to see clearly enough to count them.[1] I am not now concerned to raise the question whether Hume, having defined an impression as a perception of the mind, can consistently put forward the notion of an unperceived impression; I wish merely to point out that these exceptions which he makes prove that as a rule he regards the mind as an observer which perceives the passions which are present to it.[2]

Hume makes a distinction between the cause of a

[1] In Book I of the *Treatise*, Part 3, section 12, Hume puts forward the thesis that "a man who desires a thousand pounds has, in reality, a thousand or more desires, which, uniting together, seem to make only one passion." A man, if offered the choice of £1000 or £1001 will choose the latter; so his desire for £1001 must be greater than his desire for £1000. "Yet nothing can be more certain than that so small a difference would not be discernible in the passions, nor could render them distinguishable from each other." The solution which Hume offers to this difficulty is as follows: "The mind can perceive, from its immediate feeling, that three guineas produce a greater passion than two; and *this* it transfers to larger numbers, because of resemblance; and by a general rule assigns to a thousand guineas a stronger passion than to nine hundred and ninety-nine".

[2] Hume also speaks of the mind as having "organs" for each of the passions (*Op. cit.* II, 1, 5; II, 2, 11).

passion and the object of a passion. Discussing pride, he observes that a suit of clothes causes this passion only if it is in some way connected with oneself. "The first idea, that is presented to the mind, is that of the cause or productive principle. This excites the passion connected with it; and that passion, when excited, turns our view to another idea, which is that of self. Here then is a passion placed betwixt two ideas, of which the one produces it, and the other is produced by it. The first idea, therefore, represents the *cause*, the second the *object* of the passion" (*Op. cit.* II, 1, 2). It is natural to understand the phrase "the object of pride" as meaning *what* one is proud *of*; and Hume elsewhere talks in this way about the objects of the passions: the object of hunger is what one is hungry *for*, viz., food, and the object of lust or 'the amorous passion' is what one lusts *after*, namely sex.[1] Since one can be proud of a suit of clothes it is therefore a little surprising to find that Hume denies that this is the object of pride. Still, it is clear that Hume is pointing out that in pride whatever one is proud of makes one feel pleased with *oneself;* and perhaps we could put his point by saying that whatever expression completes the sense of the verb ". . . is proud of . . ." must begin with "his own . . .", even if what a man is proud of is only his brother-in-law's acquaintance with the second cousin of a Duke.

Thus, Hume recognizes much more clearly than Descartes that a passion is in some way connected with its object. Now is this connection, for him, contingent or necessary? "The object of pride and

---

[1] *Op. cit.* II, 1, 5; II, 2, 11. Similarly, the object of love is the person loved and the object of hatred the person hated (II, 2, 1).

humility," he writes, "is determined by an original and natural instinct and it is absolutely impossible, from the primary constitution of the mind, that these passions should ever look beyond self. . . . For this I pretend not to give any reason; but consider such a peculiar direction of the thought as an original quality" (*Op. cit.* II, 1, 5). Despite the vigour of the language it is clear that the connection here affirmed is a contingent one. It is because our minds happen to be made as they are that the object of pride is self, not because of anything involved in the concept of *pride*; just as it is because our bodies happen to be made as they are that our ears are lower than our eyes, not because of anything involved in the concept of *ear*. A passion can be, and be recognized as, pride before the idea of its object comes before the mind: the relation between the passion and this idea is one of cause and effect, and therefore, on Hume's general principles, a contingent one, inductively established. "The uniting principle among our internal perceptions is as unintelligible as that among external objects and is not known to us in any other way than by experience" (*Op. cit.* I, 3, 14). An examination of pride itself, therefore, could no more teach us that it was connected with the idea of self than an *a priori* examination of a stone could show that it would fall downward if unsupported (Cf. *Enquiry,* IV). It always happens that we feel proud of our own achievements and not, say, of the industry of ants in stone-age Papua; but the suggestion that we might feel proud of such things is as perfectly intelligible as the suggestion that the trees might flourish in December and decay in June. The idea of self is not part of the nature of pride and humility;[1] all that belongs to this is a particular experience. The "very being and essence" of these passions is "the sensations, or peculiar emotions they excite in the soul", namely a non-bodily pain and pleasure. "Thus pride is a pleasant sensation and humility a painful; and upon the removal of the pleasure and pain, there is in reality no pride nor humility. Of this our very feeling convinces us; and beyond our feeling, 'tis here in vain to reason or dispute" (*Treatise*, II, 1, 5).

The production of the passions by their causes is explained by Hume in accordance with his principles of the association of impressions and the association of ideas. Love, for instance, is an agreeable sensation which calls up the idea of some other person; it may be produced by the beauty of that person. This is because love, being a pleasant sensation, is associated by resemblance with the pleasant sensation which is caused by beauty, while the idea of this beauty is related to the idea of the person whose beauty it is, which idea represents the object of the passion of love (*Op. cit.* II, 2, 1–2). Again, by the association of impressions, one passion may give rise to another similar one. "Grief and disappointment give rise to anger, anger to envy, envy to malice, and malice to grief again, until the whole circle be completed." There are some passions, such as hunger, which are

[1] Hume denies very explicitly the intensionality of the passions in a passage in the *Treatise*, II, 3, 3. "A passion is an original existence, or, if you will, modification of existence, and contains not any representative quality, which renders it a copy of any other existence or modification. When I am angry, I am actually possessed with the passion, and in that emotion have no more a reference to any other object, than when I am thirsty, or sick, or more than five feet high."

produced by the appropriate organs without the concurrence of any external object; but the organs of pride and of lust and of many other passions, like the palate which is the organ of taste, require the assistance of some foreign object to produce any impression. All these connections between passions and their causes are, like any other causal connection, purely contingent (*Op. cit.* II, 1, 4–5).

Hume has not very much to say about the relation between a passion and its spontaneous expression in the outward bearing of the subject. But he notes that in animals there are "evident marks" of the passions: "The very port and gait of a swan, or turkey, or peacock, show the high idea he has entertained of himself, and his contempt of all others" (*Op. cit.* II, 1, 12).

On the relation between the passions and voluntary behaviour, Hume is more explicit. It is well known that he maintained that all voluntary behaviour whatsoever was motivated by passion, reason being by itself impotent to produce any action (*Op. cit.* II, 3, 3). Voluntary behaviour is behaviour which is accompanied by an indefinable internal impression called "a volition"; this in turn is caused by one or other passion. This causal relation is spoken of in several metaphorical ways; we read of "exerting passion in action," and are told that when we feel an emotion of aversion or propensity we "are carried to avoid or embrace what will give us uneasiness or satisfaction" (*Op. cit.* II, 3, 1 and 3). But the production of volition by passion is just a particular case of the production of one passion by another in accordance with the principle of association of impressions:

thus a suit of fine clothes produces pleasure from their beauty, and this pleasure produces the impression of volition (*Op. cit.* II, 3, 9). Exactly how volition in its turn effects action Hume does not and cannot well explain.

It would serve no purpose to follow Hume through his accounts of the particular passions. Like Descartes, he conceives his task to be to give a causal explanation of the origin of each emotion; though the explanations which he gives are in terms of associations of perceptions rather than bodily mechanisms, and his metaphors are drawn from chemistry rather than from clockwork. His differences from Descartes arise not from a disagreement about the nature of the passions, but from a disagreement about the nature of causality.

Like Descartes, Hume thought that the only way to learn the meaning of an emotion-word was by experiencing what it stood for. "The passions of *pride* and *humility*," he writes, "being simple and uniform impressions, it is impossible we can ever, by a multitude of words, give a just definition of them, or indeed of any of the passions. But as these words, *pride* and *humility*, are of general use, and the impressions they represent the most common of any, every one, of himself, will be able to form a just idea of them, without any danger of mistake" (*Op. cit.* II, 1, 2; Cf. II, 2, 1 and II, 3, 1).

The most significant difference between Hume and Descartes is that the former admits, while the latter denies, the possibility of the mind's making a mistake in its perception of the passions. In this, Hume is more faithful than Descartes to the picture of the relation of mind to passion as that of a sense-faculty to its object; for a sense-faculty which is in principle incapable of going wrong or failing to discriminate is inconceivable. But Descartes' view is more consistent with the principle, held by Hume no less than by himself, that a passion is an event directly observable only by the person who experiences it. It was Hume's theory which was to prevail. Since it was stated by some empirical psychologists more explicitly than by Hume himself, I shall postpone criticism of it to a later place.

CHAPTER TWO

THE EXPERIMENTAL EXAMINATION
OF THE EMOTIONS

WHEN in the nineteenth century men first en-
deavoured to construct an experimental science
of psychology, they accepted uncriticised many of the
presuppositions common to Descartes and Hume.
Some, believing that an emotion was the object of an
inward perception, concluded that the study of the
emotions could be made scientific only by training
introspectors in precise observation and accurate
measurement of their interior states. Thus were
devised series of 'introspective experiments' designed
to secure ever more detailed and precise descriptions
of internal impressions. Wundt, Titchener, and their
disciples, for example, tried to settle *how many*
emotions there are by applying various stimuli to
laboratory subjects and asking for their introspective
reports. A textbook recently in use remarks: "The
observer in an introspective experiment on feeling
needs to adopt a special attitude to the situation
which is presented him. Rather than perceiving the
situation and dealing actively with it, he must im-
merse himself in it and live it, at the same time trying
to observe the emotional experience which comes over

29

him."[1] One subject, for instance, given a piece of chocolate, produced this report: "The characterization, pleasant, applies to the experienced complex, the predominant components of which were the quality of sweet and a brightness or lightness reminiscent of bright pressure."[2]

The presuppositions of this type of experiment are clearly Cartesian. An emotion is regarded as an experience only contingently connected with its manifestation: no essential part of it is lost if the normal behaviour characteristic of it is replaced by a quite special laboratory attitude of 'immersion in experience'. Emotion-words are conceived as names for particular features of experience: the subject of the sample report clearly thought that his task was to discover by close inward attention exactly what feature of experience the word "pleasant" named.

Introspective experiments are no longer so fashionable; but the Cartesian presuppositions remain influential. Hebb, for instance, no great believer in the value of introspective reports, can yet write in a recent book "Private, or subjective, or introspective evidence concerns events within the observer himself, and by the nature of things available to that one observer. ... Speech, and introspective description, is not a sort of pipeline direct to the consciousness of another, giving us first-hand knowledge. It is behaviour, from which we may infer, correctly or incorrectly, the nature of the underlying processes that determined what the subject has said. All that we can

[1] Woodworth, *Experimental Psychology*, Chapter X.
[2] "Bright pressure" was a technical phrase of Titchener's laboratory; it meant something "not far removed from tickle".

know about the conscious processes of another, or about what the psychiatrist calls the unconscious, is *an inference from behaviour*, verbal or nonverbal" (*A Textbook of Psychology*, 4).

Like Descartes, Hebb thinks that there are conscious processes which can be observed only by their subject and which others can know only by inference; unlike Descartes, he thinks that introspective reports of these processes are extremely fallible.[1] It is hard to see how he can consistently do so. If these events are 'available to the observer only', how can any one else ever get into a position to correct the observer? Perhaps the observer himself may say something later which will contradict his earlier report: but in that case, why take his report after the event as more reliable than his report at the time? It may be that an introspective observer will say two inconsistent things in quick succession: as a man may say that he has a picture in his mind's eye of a page of poetry, and then admit that he cannot read this page backwards (*Op. cit.*, 35). Hebb takes such a case as evidence that the observer had misreported a visual process which is quite genuinely going on in his mind. But why, on his principles, should we not say that this visual process has changed its nature between the observer's first report and his later admission? If the process is something which the subject alone can observe, then what he says at any moment is the best possible evidence for the nature of the process at that moment. But if his statement is the best possible

[1] "A subject's reports may be a most unreliable source of information about what goes on in the mind of another, even though he is entirely honest" (*Op. cit.*, 4).

evidence for what happens in his mind, then it cannot be corrected; for statements can be corrected only in the light of better evidence about the topic which they concern. But where an utterance is of a kind which cannot in principle be corrected, there is no room for a distinction between its being right or wrong, or being a more or less reliable report. The whole project, therefore, of training introspectors in greater accuracy in the observation of their internal states was misconceived; for in this context we can attach no sense to "accuracy".

Introspectors were sometimes asked by psychologists not only to pronounce on the nature of their inner emotions, but also to estimate their quantity. For a thoroughgoing introspectionist, the best possible evidence of the intensity, as of the nature, of an emotion is provided by the subject's own report. Flugel, for instance, asked nine subjects to record, almost hourly for a month, the quality and intensity of their feelings, marking them on a numerical scale from $+3$ for intense pleasure to -3 for intense un-pleasure. He correlated the records carefully and published the results (which he did not find entirely satisfactory) with a wealth of statistical sophistication in a paper entitled *A Quantitative Study of Feeling and Emotion in Everyday Life.*[1]

Flugel's purpose in this study was to discover whether human life was on the whole more pleasant than painful.[2] What people are inclined to say about them is certainly one of the criteria which we use for

[1] *Studies in Feeling and Desire*, 155–194.

[2] His conclusion, the reader may be reassured to learn, was that it was.

32

assessing the intensity of emotional states; Flugel's mistake lay in attributing to these utterances the status of uniquely privileged reports.[1] He did indeed come to doubt the reliability of some of the reports, and confessed that the records "leave much to be desired from the point of view of scientific accuracy". As we have shown, this is something which, on his introspectionist principles, he can have no right to say. There can never be any reason to impugn the accuracy of a measurement which is made by the only person in a position to measure at the only time at which measurement is possible. Flugel thought that he had collected inaccurate reports of all-important private data; what he had in fact collected were public data of a comparatively unimportant kind.

There are other methods of assessing the intensity of emotions besides taking note of what people say. Some of them concern phenomena which are capable of the precise measurement which seemed to many psychologists essential if the study of the emotions was to be made into an exact science. Feelings of rage and terror, for example, are accompanied by bodily changes, some of which (such as facial contortions) are observable by the layman, while others (such as the psychogalvanic reflex) can be detected only with the aid of apparatus. Many of the bodily changes characteristic of the various emotions have been patiently and precisely investigated by psycho-

---

[1] He wrote that the only hope of obtaining reliable information with regard to his problem "would seem to lie in the resort to the more precise methods of introspection and evaluation that have been developed by experimental psychology" (*Op. cit.*, 156).

logists during the course of this century.[1] A well-known example of this sort of work was Blatz's study of fear made in 1925. A trick chair in his laboratory tilted blindfold subjects unexpectedly backwards, while their breathing was recorded on a pneumograph and the rate and force of their heartbeat on an electro-cardiograph. When the chair was tilted, the subject's pulse-rate shot up, and the force and rate of his heartbeat increased.[2] Other workers investigated correlations between emotional states and brain-frequencies, visceral activities and glandular secretions. Many studies were made of the manifestation of emotion by the psychogalvanic reflex (the lowering of the electrical resistance of the skin in response to stimulation). Words and phrases, loud noises, electric shocks, films and stories were used as stimuli to produce emotion in subjects whose PGR was measured and recorded.[3]

Because all these phenomena could be accurately observed and precisely measured, there was a temptation to experimental psychologists to pretend that in measuring these phenomena they were measuring emotion. It was true that there were many emotions, such as hope and love and vanity, which did not seem to be patient of this type of investigation. It was true also that fears of certain objects, such as a world war or a wet bank holiday, did not seem to be so

[1] The two classic accounts of work in this field are *Bodily Changes in Pain, Hunger, Fear and Rage,* by W. B. Cannon, and *Emotions and Bodily Changes,* by F. Dunbar.

[2] Blatz, "The cardiac, respiratory and electrical phenomena involved in the emotion of fear"—*J. Exper. Psychol.* 1925.

[3] Woodworth gives an account of several such experiments in Chapter XIII of his *Experimental Psychology.*

intimately connected with bodily changes as the fear of falling or of burning one's fingers with a lighted match. Such cases, however, seem to have been regarded as degenerate cases of emotion. Chronic fears, it seems to have been thought, differed from sudden frights merely in being less intense and therefore less perceptible specimens of the emotion.

There is an insoluble objection to this way of looking at the matter. It is indeed true that emotions admit of degrees of intensity. Anger can be slight or violent, fears strong or weak; one man's love may be greater than another's, and jealousy can wax and wane. But if we look for the criterion of the intensity of an emotion, we find not one but two criteria, which may on occasion conflict. The first criterion is the violence of the bodily changes, of facial expression, tone of voice, posture, gesture, and so forth, which are associated with the emotion. It is this criterion which is extended and made more precise by the psychologists' investigations into the physiological states which correlate with the obvious verbal and behavioural expressions of emotion. But there is another criterion also. We may regard one emotion as stronger than another if it has a greater influence on voluntary action over a comparatively long period of time. On this criterion, how powerful an emotion is depends on how much of a man's behaviour can be explained by reference to it.

The distinction between these criteria of intensity seems to correspond to a distinction which we may make between emotion as feeling and emotion as motive. The vehemence of a feeling of rage will be most appropriately measured by the first method, the strength of ambition as a motive by the second. Even where one and the same emotion is in question, different methods will be appropriate to different objects of emotion. The intensity of a fear of snakes may be measured by the first method; the strength of a fear of inflation only by the second. In general, where emotions are immediate reactions to present stimuli, such as animals may display, the first method of measurement will be natural; where the object of an emotion is something distant in space or time or something which only a language-user could appreciate, the second method will be the more appropriate, and often the only possible, one.

There are, however, cases where fear of one and the same object may be measurable by both methods. Fear of heights, for instance, might be measured either by the violence of the bodily phenomena occurring when the subject is placed on a height, or by the amount of trouble which he will take to avoid having to stand on exposed high places. If we measure a man's fear of heights by the number of times in his life he has feelings of such fear, we shall obtain a result quite contrary to that which we obtain if we measure the strength of the fear by the effect which it has on his behaviour. A man who is very afraid of heights will never climb mountains, ascend towers, or look over beetling cliffs, and so will very rarely display the feelings of fear which heights cause. On the other hand, a mountaineer may sometimes suffer from sinking stomach, incipient trembling, and a watery sensation in the knees, without thereby being frightened off an ascent. When both come to die, the mountain-climber's biography will contain more records of feelings of fear of heights than that of the man who was timidly anchored to sea-level.

There may indeed be a certain correlation between estimates of the intensity of an emotion obtained in these two different ways. It may be that the man who takes most pains to avoid heights is also the man who will show the most violent bodily symptoms of fear if he is taken against his will to the top of a precipice. But the bodily symptoms thus experimentally induced are in a sense no longer the natural manifestation of the fear of heights; for by taking the subject against his will to an exposed high place we have deprived his fear of its most natural expression.

It is obvious that the measurement of the strength of an emotion as a motive could never be made precise in the way in which psychologists attempted to make precise the measurement of emotional feelings. A motive is strong if it governs prolonged or dramatic tracts of a man's behaviour; its intensity is measured by the frequency and importance of actions done out of it. But we cannot devise apparatus to measure the number and importance of human actions as we can record the frequency and strength of a man's heart-beats with a cardiograph.[1]

It follows from the impossibility of precise measure-

[1] Even with animals, there is a certain artificiality in attempting to give precise quantitative estimates of the strengths of motives ("measures of drive"). For the mathematical results obtained may differ if different measurable phenomena are taken as the criterion of strength for the motive. The strength of hunger in rats in a Skinner box, for example, may be measured either by the rate at which they will press a lever for small amounts of nutrient solution, or by the amount of food which they will ingest. Both criteria have been used by different experimenters (cf. Deutsch, *The Structural Basis of Behaviour*, 21 and 166).

ments of the strength of motives that it is also impossible in principle to make precise measurements of the intensity of emotional feelings. For it is not just an unfortunate accident of idiom that we use the same words, such as "love", "anger", and "fear", in the description of feelings as we do in the attribution of motives. The two uses of an emotion-word are two exercises of a single concept; for it is through their connection with motivated behaviour that feelings are identified as feelings of a particular emotion. The precisely measurable bodily phenomena which psychologists study are not identical with the feelings of which they are characteristic; for unlike the feelings they have a merely contingent connection with motivated behaviour. There is a conceptual connection also between a feeling and its object, whereas the physiological processes studied by psychologists lack intensionality. Bodily changes may be the vehicle of an emotion, but they are not themselves emotion. As Aristotle said, a man who defines anger as a bubbling of the blood about the heart gives only the matter without the form (*De Anima*, 403 a 29).

These conceptual points were sometimes neglected by investigators, and sometimes brought home to them by their own experimental results.[1] For instance, it

[1] Ruckmick, for example, claims that the intensionality of anger is an experimental discovery. He writes: "Most writers agree that objectless emotions are impossible. In numerous investigations in the psychological laboratory of the University of Iowa on *bona fide* anger, produced under experimental conditions, the observations clearly show that this among other emotions is always directed either towards the experimenter, towards the observer himself, who feels responsible for getting himself in this situation, or towards the physical conditions which have provoked the anger" (*The Psychology of Feeling and Emotion*, 66). Hebb likewise claims it as an

soon became clear that many of the somatic phenomena characteristic of particular emotions occurred
also in connection with quite different emotions. The
respiratory and cardiac changes recorded by Blatz
in his experiments on fear occurred also, with differences only in degree, when the experimental subjects
paid a second visit to the tilting chair, though neither
they nor the experimenter were then prepared to
describe their feelings as feelings of fear. The psychogalvanic reflex was found to occur with varying
intensity in any sort of excitement, from startle to
sexual pleasure.[1] Were we to identify the emotions
with bodily phenomena of this kind, we should have
to say that shame differed from rage in degree and not
in kind, and that a feeling of apprehension, if it grew
stronger, would turn into passionate love.

William James, as is well known, identified the
emotions not with bodily processes themselves but
with the perception of these processes.

Our natural way of thinking about coarser emotions is
that the mental perception of some fact excites the mental
affection called the emotion, and that this latter state of
mind gives rise to the bodily expression. My theory, on
the contrary, is that *the bodily changes follow directly
the perception of the exciting fact, and that our feeling of
the same changes as they occur IS the emotion.* Commonsense says, we lose our fortune, are sorry and weep; we
meet a bear, are frightened and run; we are insulted by a
rival, are angry and strike. The hypothesis here to be
defended says that this order of sequence is incorrect,

[1] Woodworth, *Experimental Psychology*, Chapter XIII.

empirical discovery that introspection is not the best method of
learning about mental states (*A Textbook of Psychology*, 266).

that the one mental state is not immediately induced by the other, that the bodily manifestations must first be interposed between, and that the more rational statement is that we feel sorry because we cry, angry because we strike, afraid because we tremble (*The Principles of Psychology*, Dover Edn., II, 450).

James's theory, we have already noted, was anticipated by Descartes; and it is open to some of the general objections against the Cartesian system. For James the emotions are states so private that the conclusive verification of his theory can come only from introspection.[1] The relation between emotions and their expression is still a causal one even though the causal order usually suggested is reversed.

The theory, however, runs into special difficulties of its own. In order to account for the great variety of emotional states, James insisted that there was hardly any limit to the permutations and combinations of possible minute bodily changes. Moreover, he had to claim "that *every one of the bodily changes, whatsoever it be, is FELT, acutely or obscurely, the moment it occurs*" (*Op. cit.*, 451). Now what is the criterion for the occurrence of such a feeling of minute bodily change? If it is the non-verbal behaviour of the subject, then it must be his display of emotion, which *ex hypothesi* is his only behaviour at the relevant time. But if so, then James is merely renaming the emotions

[1] *Op. cit.* II, 451, 455. It might be thought that by identifying emotion with the perception of bodily states, James was linking emotion non-contingently to its expression. But given James's causal theory of perception, this is not so. "A purely disembodied human emotion is a nonentity. I do not say that it is a contradiction in the nature of things, or that pure spirits are necessarily condemned to cold intellectual lives" (*Op. cit.*, 452).

"perceptions of bodily changes" and his theory has no explanatory force. If on the other hand the criterion is the verbal behaviour of the subject—what he can say —then the theory is obviously false. One of the bodily changes in fear, we are told, is the increased secretion of the adrenal glands. On James's theory, fear consists partly in the perception of this secretion. But people felt fear long before the adrenals were heard of; and if nowadays we can sometimes infer the state of our adrenals from the state of our feelings, we infer the secretion from the fear, not the fear from the secretion. In fact James suggests no criterion, and sees no need for one: the feeling of a bodily change is clearly for him an internal impression, which carries its specification on its face.

In support of his theory, James pleads that it is impossible to have any strong emotion without having the appropriate bodily sensations.[1] But this, if true, no more proves that an emotion is identical with bodily sensations than the fact that sums are done with symbols proves that numbers are identical with numerals.

The most vociferous of James's critics were the behaviourists. The behaviourists accepted the prevailing identification of feelings with Cartesian private events; rightly rejecting Cartesian private events, they wrongly concluded that there were no such things

---

[1] It is not clear whether James puts this forward as an argument or as an invitation to conduct an introspective experiment. He tells us to "fancy some strong emotion and then try to abstract from our consciousness of it all the feelings of its bodily symptoms" and says that "most people say that their introspection verifies" his theory; but later he says that the task proposed is a "purely speculative one" of abstracting certain elements in an imagined state and describing what remains (*Op. cit.*, 452).

D

as feelings. Accepting the currently over-simplified view of the relation between a name and what it names, they thought that since a word like "fear" was not the name of an introspectible sensation, it must be the name of a publicly observable reaction.

Watson, the founder of behaviourism, devoted most of his work on the emotions to studies designed to discover which emotional reactions in children were inherited and which were learnt. As a result of his experiments he came to the conclusion that there were three main types of unconditioned stimuli producing emotional reactions in children. Loud sounds and sudden loss of support produced checking of the breath, crying, a start of the whole body, and marked visceral responses; holding or restraint produced crying with open mouth, prolonged holding of breath, reddening of face, etc.; stroking the skin, and especially the sex-organs, produced smiling, cessation of crying, changes in respiration, cooing, gurgling, erection, and other visceral changes. These three behaviour patterns, he suggested, are the starting points from which are built up the complicated conditioned habit patterns which we call the emotions of fear, rage, and love. The complication of adult emotional life is achieved by an increase in the number of stimuli, due to conditioning and transfers, and additions and modifications to the responses (*Behaviourism*, Phoenix Books Edn., 155–165).

There are two difficulties about accepting Watson's work as a complete account of the emotions. The first concerns the description of the response itself. There are many adult expressions of fear and love which correspond in no detail to the behaviour described by Watson. An executive who drops into a pillar-box a cheque to a blackmailer and a love-letter to his mistress is performing at the same time two actions, one out of fear and one out of love; yet he need not be crying, starting, smiling, holding his breath, cooing, gurgling, or suffering visceral commotions, and indeed he can hardly be doing all these things at the same time. The adult behaviour is not merely 'an addition and modification' to the infant pattern described; it is, considered just as a piece of behaviour, a totally different response. Watson admits that the stimuli in the adult case may be very dissimilar to the unconditioned stimuli; a letter from a blackmailer is not very like a loud noise or a sudden withdrawal of support. But where stimulus and response are *both* totally different, what grounds have we for talking of the *same* behaviour pattern at all? Watson does indeed feel misgivings, He says: "While I use the words fear, rage, and love, I want to strip them of all their old connotations. Please look upon the reactions we designate by them just as you look upon breathing, heartbeat, and grasping. . . . Probably we should not call these reactions fear, rage, and love, but rather reactions X, Y, and Z." Had he followed this programme consistently, one would have no fault to find with him; but then, of course, there could have been no suggestion that an understanding of reactions X, Y, and Z in children might suffice for an understanding of reactions A, B, and C in adults, which also happen to be called "fear", "love", and "rage". In fact, Watson's arguments repeatedly demand that one should understand "fear" in its ordinary sense; as when he makes deductions from his experiments on 'reaction X' about the desirability of inducing fear of punishment in children.

The second difficulty concerns the relation between the description of the response and the description of the stimulus. Even the infantile responses are recognizable as emotional responses only when we know the stimuli which called them forth. If, therefore, fear is a response, it is a response which has a more than contingent connection with its stimulus. But where this seems to be the case, it is a sure sign that the stimulus-response pattern is not the correct one to apply.

Wittgenstein once suggested that we should forget for a moment that we are interested in, e.g., the state of mind of a frightened man. We should still have an interest in observing a man's behaviour under certain circumstances, as an indication of his future conduct. We might well have a verb for this: a verb which would lack a first-person use. Even such a verb, Wittgenstein insisted, would not simply be a designation of behaviour or bodily changes: it would refer to behaviour *in certain external circumstances*.

The investigation of the emotions is not regarded by psychologists themselves as one of the fields in which experimental methods have been most successful. To conclude our discussion of the logical problems involved in such investigation, it may help to consider recent studies in an allied field—that of need—where experimental methods have produced clear answers to clear questions, and where technical dexterity has not been lamed by conceptual confusion.[1]

[1] Even here there have been some muddles: see Deutsch's just criticism of Hull's 'intervening variables' (*The Structural Basis of Behaviour*, 4–5).

The behaviour of animals under conditions of need is particularly suitable for experimental investigation since "need" can be defined without any reference to the behaviour of the animal concerned. Being a concept which applies also to plants and artefacts, *need* can be explained purely by reference to the conditions necessary for the survival or normal functioning of the entity in question. Thus Hull defines "need" in the following way: "Organisms require on the whole a rather precise set of conditions for optimal chances of individual and species survival. When these conditions deviate appreciably from the optimum, a state of need is said to exist."[1] The needs most commonly investigated by psychologists are the need for food (and for particular substances such as salt and sugar) and water: the needs associated with hunger and thirst. The need for food is not, of course, *the same thing* as hunger, nor is the need for water *the same thing* as thirst. Hunger and thirst are non-contingently connected with eating and drinking, whereas the connection between particular bodily deficiencies and particular types of behaviour is established by observation (not necessarily of a recondite kind). Plants may need water but plants cannot be thirsty.

There are three theories current to explain the behaviour of animals under conditions of need; those of Hull, of Tinbergen and Lorenz, and of Deutsch. All three theories agree that there is a causal connection between the existence of a state of need and the initiation of behaviour of a kind apt to remove the

[1] *Essentials of Behaviour*, 15; quoted in Deutsch, *op. cit.* 17. The words ". . . and species . . ." are questionable (*Ibid.*, 19).

need. The theories differ in their account of the mechanism by which this consummatory behaviour is continued and finally stopped. According to Hull, the activity lasts as long as the need and ceases when the need ceases; according to the Tinbergen-Lorenz hypothesis the duration of the activity is proportionate to the intensity and duration of the need prior to the initiation of activity; according to Deutsch, the cessation of activity depends in large measure on further stimulation independent of the original need.[1]

There is experimental evidence for and against each of these hypotheses. In favour of Hull's thesis is the observed fact that a dog will eat far more than its normal requirement if it is so operated on that no food reaches its stomach; against it is the fact that eating, in general, stops long before the processes of digestion are complete. In favour of the Tinbergen-Lorenz view is the experiment of Bellows, which showed that dogs with an esophageal fistula drank only the amount of water they would have done had water been reaching their stomach; against it is the fact established by Kohn and others that animals when nourished artificially other than by eating will exhibit less food-seeking behaviour than when not so nourished. Deutsch's theory is supported by the observations of Smith, who showed that it was possible to reduce the food intake of rats by direct stimulation of the hypothalamus without any reduction of need; it finds

[1] Deutsch postulates receptoral systems (e.g. in the stomach) which when stimulated switch off the link which, under stimulation from the internal environment, has initiated the appropriate behaviour (e.g. eating). *Op. cit.*, 33–34.

difficulty in accounting for the results obtained by Miller and others who found that drinking in rats could be cut off by the injection of water directly into the stomach (whereas the receptors whose stimulation Deutsch believes to effect the cessation of drinking are situated in the throat).[1]

It would be quite out of place to offer any suggestion about the relative merits of these hypotheses; the point of philosophical interest is that here we have a set of problems capable of formulation in ways which make them soluble by experimental methods. The structures postulated by the various theories are not only indirectly inferable from the behaviour of animals, but are capable of direct experimental investigation: Verney, Anderson, McCann, and others have tentatively identified the components of the central nervous system sensitive to particular chemical states which are postulated by all three hypotheses. But, as Deutsch rightly observes, the value of a theory such as his own is to a great extent independent of the discovery of the exact location and nature of the physiological elements in which the structure he postulates is realized.

Now would it be possible to devise experiments to investigate mechanisms operative in emotion in the way in which these psychologists have investigated the mechanisms operative in hunger and thirst? It seems not, for the following reasons. We have seen that there is no bodily state which stands in the same relation to emotional behaviour as the states of need stand in relation to hungry and thirsty behaviour.

[1] The experimental evidence is summarized in Deutsch, *op. cit.* 17–34.

47

Bodily states are not identified as states of need by the fact that they are followed by the appropriate behaviour: the whole procedure of experimental investigation consists in varying the natural relations between the two separately identifiable phenomena of need-reduction and consummatory activity. But bodily states are identified as states of a particular emotion partly by their connection with motivated behaviour and (in man) with the verbal expressions of emotion.

There is, again, no particular form of behaviour which is characteristic of an emotion in the way in which eating is characteristic of hunger. The form which emotional behaviour takes is dependent on the object of the emotion in question. So that even if a particular bodily state could be identified with a particular emotion, we know in advance that we could not identify any mechanism which connected this bodily state with a particular form of behaviour.

But bodily states cannot be identified with emotions. It is true that emotions may be affected by treatment of bodily states, and that bodily states may be changed by the talking away of an emotion; as benzedrine may cure depression, and pre-examination diarrhœa be brought to an end by words of encouragement. None the less, a bodily state is not *qua* bodily state an emotional state; for it is only if it occurs in the appropriate circumstances that we can call it an emotional state at all.

A state of need can be identified as such no matter how it has been caused; it is not so with emotional states, and hence there is a special difficulty about producing them in laboratory conditions. If a chemist wishes to investigate the nature of an acid, it does not in general matter how he obtains it; whether it is produced naturally or artificially, whether he manufactures it himself or buys it from a supplier. This is because it is no part of the criterion of a substance's being an acid of such-and-such a kind that it should have been produced in such-and-such circumstances. No matter how it has been produced, provided that it possesses in purity the defining properties of its kind, it is a suitable specimen for investigation. When the psychologist investigates an emotion it is not so. The occasion on which an emotion is elicited is part of the criterion for the nature of the emotion. Merely to investigate behaviour or its physiological accompaniments, without reference to the occasions on which these occur, is to treat something which is essential to establishing the nature of what is being investigated as if it was a dispensable laboratory circumstance. The tears which we shed while watching films, the shudders which we give while reading horror stories are real tears and real shudders; but the surroundings are not those of real grief or real horror. We do not want the film to stop, or put the book down.

However, there have been laboratory experiments on genuine as well as *ersatz* emotions, in which, for example, fear was elicited in the face of real danger. Now danger is identifiable quite separately from danger-avoiding behaviour, just as need is identifiable independently of need-reducing behaviour. Have we not therefore in danger and fear-behaviour two independent variables to correspond to the independent variables of need and consummatory activity? Let us note first that we could not postulate special danger-receptors in the nervous system as psychologists postulate receptors sensitive to changes in the blood-stream; for it seems obvious that a dog sees dangerous objects with the same eyes as it sees food. Still, this difficulty can be got over by learning-theory; there is another which is not so tractable. For an animal to be genuinely afraid, it is not necessary nor sufficient that he should be in danger; he may be in danger which he does not know about, and so not afraid, or be in no danger, but be afraid because he thinks he is. No similar complication arises about need: an animal is in need if his body is in a certain condition, no matter what the animal 'thinks' about it. But now the two 'independent variables' become: the *belief in* danger, and fear-behaviour. And what criterion could we have for attributing to an animal a belief in danger other than his fear-behaviour itself?

Earlier, I insisted that fear was recognized as such partly by means of the external circumstances in which it occurred. It may now seem inconsistent that I have admitted that an animal might show fear though it was in no danger. The inconsistency is only apparent; the external circumstances necessary are not necessarily dangerous circumstances, but there must be something in the environment to serve as a target for the animal's fear: say, some physical object which he avoids, or a certain time at which he grows restless because he has been conditioned by receiving a shock at a precise interval after a stimulus. Without some such circumstance no behaviour would be recognizable as fear-behaviour, and no bodily state could be called a state of fear.

All this is in no way meant to deny that there are physical processes connecting the bodily states characteristic of the emotions with the physiological events connected with the perception of a particular emotional stimulus and with the exhibition of particular forms of emotional behaviour. The investigation of these processes may well lead to results of the highest interest; but it can not have the status of an experimental examination of the nature of the emotions.

CHAPTER THREE

FEELINGS

THE notion of an 'inner sense' which perceives the perceiver's emotions is lent plausibility by the use of the verb "to feel" in reports both of emotional states and of perceptions. We feel compassion, and we feel lumps in the mattress; we feel pangs of remorse and we feel pokes in the ribs. This makes it natural to think that compassion and pangs of remorse are things which are perceived by those who suffer them, as lumps in the mattress and pokes in the ribs are perceived by those on whom they are inflicted.

Grammatically, there are at least three constructions which are used after the verb "to feel". Sometimes, the verb has a direct object, as when we speak of feeling an itch, feeling the smoothness of satin, feeling our way, feeling inconvenience. In other cases the verb is followed, as the verb "to be" often is, simply by an adjective which it is natural to regard as qualifying the subject of the verb: as when we say that someone feels cold, or sick, or lonely, or anxious. In a third set of cases the verb is followed by an *oratio obliqua* clause, whether of the "*that* ..." form (as in "feeling that the moment was unpropitious") or of the 'accusative and infinitive' form (as in "feeling the

moment to be unpropitious"). Besides these main
constructions after "to feel" there are other idiomatic
uses such as "feeling oneself", "feeling up to . . .",
"feeling like" (in the two different senses of "feeling
like a lord" and "feeling like a drink"), "feeling in
good spirits". Sometimes the verb is used quite on its
own; as in Wordsworth's "the meanest thing that
feels".

Not all of these grammatical constructions are of
philosophical importance. In Latin, for instance, the
second construction would be impossible: "*Balbus
sentit aeger*" would earn few marks as a translation
of "Balbus feels ill". In English, too, we can frequently
express exactly the same thought in more than one of
these constructions. Thus, one can feel cold or feel the
cold; feel hungry or feel hunger; feel lonely or feel
loneliness. The slight differences of nuance between
the members of these pairs of expressions are of no
interest to the philosopher.

What is of interest to him is the difference between
the cases where such translation between constructions is possible, and those where it is not. To feel
anger may be to feel angry, but to feel a lump is not
to feel lumpish. Feeling fear does not differ from feeling
afraid, but feeling the earth is not at all the same as
feeling earthy. Again, to feel the heat of the fire is not
the same as to feel hot because of the fire, since one can
feel the heat of the fire without feeling hot. "He felt
the roughness of the stone" does not even look as if it
meant "He felt rough because of the stone". Thus it
is only in some cases that expressions in the first of the
forms listed above may be translated into expressions
of the second form.

On the other hand, expressions of the first form, the verb-and-object form, always imply expressions of the third form, the *oratio obliqua* form, whenever they cannot be translated into the second form, which we may call the quasi-copula form. Thus, to feel the lump in the mattress is to feel that there is a lump in the mattress; to feel the heat of the fire is to feel that the fire is hot; to feel the hostility of the audience is to feel that the audience is hostile, and to feel the lateness of the hour is to feel that the hour is late. (The converse does not hold: one may feel that the audience is hostile without feeling the hostility of the audience, if the audience is not hostile and one feels mistakenly that it is.) On the other hand, where expressions of the verb-and-object form admit of translation into the quasi-copula form, they do not admit of translation into expressions of the *oratio obliqua* form. If one feels guilt, then one feels guilty; but it does not follow that one feels that one is guilty, for one may regard one's guilt-feeling as the quite irrational consequence of an innocent action, due perhaps to a hangover from childish tabus. If one feels anger, then one feels angry; but it does not follow that one feels that one is angry, for one may imagine that one is being particularly cool-headed.

The distinction which we have drawn between those reports of feelings in which the direct object is replaceable by an adjective, and those in which it corresponds to a that-clause, enables us to see through the *prima facie* similarity between emotions and perceptions. But it does not by itself provide a criterion for distinguishing feelings of emotion from all other feelings. Hunger is not an emotion, though to feel

hunger is to feel hungry and is not necessarily to feel
that one is hungry (for one may mistake a feeling of
hunger for the symptom of an illness, or feel hungry
when one knows that one is in no need of food.)
So, too, with thirst, seasickness, itches, nausea, and
giddiness. In general, therefore, our criterion distinguishes between emotions and sensations on the
one hand, and perceptions on the other. It does not, in
general, distinguish between emotions and sensations.
Oddly enough, in the case of pleasure and pain, which
are sometimes sensations and sometimes emotions, the
substitutibility of the quasi-copula form for the direct-
object form does provide a criterion of distinction. To
feel sexual pleasure is not necessarily to feel pleased
about anything, but to feel pleasure at a compliment
is to feel pleased by it. To feel a pain in one's toe is not
necessarily to feel pained by anything, but to feel
pain at a friend's treachery is to feel pained about it.
In each case we have, on the one hand, a sensation,
and on the other an emotion.

The assimilation of emotions to perceptions was not,
of course, based solely on the grammatical similarity
of "I feel anger" to "I feel the money in my pocket".
There are genuine enough analogies between feelings
of emotion and the objects of the senses. A feeling of
anger, like a sound, may last for a longer or shorter
time; it may come and go suddenly, like a flash, or
last all day like the taste of onions. Distress, like
banging, may be faint or unbearable, may grow more
or less intense. There can be an emotion that is half
way between fear and curiosity, as there can be a
colour that is half way between red and blue. Duration, intensity, and blending are properties shared by

feelings of all kinds, whether perceptions, sensations, or emotions.

Emotions, unlike perceptions, do not give us any information about the external world. We can say "I know there was a policeman there, because I saw a flash of blue", but not "I know there was a policeman there, because I felt a wave of hatred". Nor do they give us information about our own bodies quite as sensations do: I may learn that I have cut myself by feeling pain, but not by feeling foolish, though my cutting myself may give rise to both these feelings. Still, one *can* learn facts about oneself from emotions: I may realise that I am drunk because I find even that old bore in the corner amusing; and a pang of jealousy may be my first clear indication that I am in love.

But the dissimilarities between emotions and perceptions are more significant than the similarities. There are not organs of emotion as there are organs of perception. We see with our eyes, smell with our noses, hear with our ears; there are no parts of our bodies with which we fear or hope or feel jealous or excited. There are indeed sensations which are characteristic of different emotions, and these sensations are frequently localized: the lump in the throat, the flutter in the stomach, the melting in the bowels. For all that, we do not feel grief with our throats, nor excitement with our stomachs, nor do we yearn with our bowels. To say that a sensation is localized in a particular part of the body is not to say that that part of the body is the organ of the sensation in question. We do not see colours in our eyes or smell odours in our noses; nor, if we are hearing genuine sounds, do we hear them in our ears. In general, to sense something *in* a part of one's body is not at all the same as to sense something *with* a part of one's body. Quite the contrary: what is sensed with an organ is never a sensation *in* one's body at all.

On the other hand, not every part of the body which is necessary for a particular mode of perception is an organ of perception. Damage to the visual area of the cortex will make a man blind; for all that, the cortex is not an organ of sight as the eye is. What then *is* an organ of perception? The concept is not entirely precise; but it seems that we shall not be far wrong if we say that an organ of perception is a part of the body which can be moved at will in ways which affect the efficiency of the sense in question. Thus, part of what is involved in the concept of sense-organ is expressed in such remarks as "You can see it if you look through this crack". "You can hear them if you put your ear to the wall". "If you don't like the smell, then hold your nose".

In this sense of 'organ', there are no organs of emotion. There is no part of one's body which one can bring to bear in order to fear better, in the way in which one can screw up one's eyes in order to see better. One does not have to get into the best position for feeling remorse, as one may have to seek out the best position for listening to a quartet. No part of one's body needs to be trained and conditioned for dog-hating, as one's palate has to be educated and prepared for wine-tasting.

Emotions, in lacking organs, are distinguished from perceptions of colour, taste, smell, heat, roughness, smoothness and all else which can be felt with a specific part of one's body. But they are not, in this,

E

distinguished from internal sensations of pain or tickle or heart-throb. Though I feel pain *in* my tooth it is not *with* my tooth, nor with anything else, that I feel pain; I may feel my heart beating, but neither my heart nor any other part of my body is an organ of this feeling. My stomach is the seat of my hunger, and the organ of my digestion; but it is not the organ of my hunger.

None the less, emotions differ from sensations. Emotions are not localized as pain, hunger and thirst are. If I have a painful sensation in my toe, then I feel a pain in my toe; but if I have a craven sensation in my stomach, this does not mean that I feel fear in my stomach. It is impossible to imagine hunger in the throat, thirst in the foot, or the discomfort of constipation in the cheek; the emotions are not in the same way linked with parts of the body. We do indeed localize emotions, but in the features of others, not in our own bodies. We say not "I felt terror in my midriff" or "I felt shame in my cheeks" but "I saw the horror in his eyes" and "you could see delight written on his face."

In some ways, bodily sensations stand half-way between perceptions and emotions. All feelings have duration; but perceptions and sensations are much more closely tied than emotions to the time which is the measure of local motion. One can hear a loud noise just for a second, or feel violent pain only for a moment, no matter what precedes or follows; one cannot in the same way feel ardent love, or deep grief for the space of a second, no matter what preceded or followed this second.[1] This is not because it takes

[1] Wittgenstein, *Philosophical Investigations*, I, 583; II, i.

longer to feel love or grief than it does to feel pain, in the way in which it takes longer to see *Gone with the Wind* than it does to see a Disney cartoon.

On the other hand, bodily sensations are like emotions in being linked with characteristic forms of expression. Hunger is linked with food-seeking behaviour and thirst with drink-seeking behaviour; there are no similarly specific forms of behaviour characteristic of seeing and hearing. We do indeed tell the difference between blind and sighted people, and between deaf people and those with normal hearing, by observing differences in their behaviour; but we do so not so much by noticing one particular pattern of behaviour which they lack, as by noticing a particular inefficiency in their behaviour generally. In being thus linked with specific forms of behaviour, sensations are closer to emotions. Hunger and thirst, however, unlike anger or fright, do not have characteristic facial expressions or tones of voice; here pain is closer to the emotions than other sensations are. But the existence of characteristic expressions of emotion itself provides a further link between emotion and sensations: for the expression characteristic of each emotion—e.g. weeping—is itself *felt*, and this feeling is a genuine sensation.

Emotions have not only a characteristic expression but also, we might say, a characteristic history.

"Grief" describes a pattern which recurs, with different variations, in the weave of our life. If a man's bodily expression of sorrow and of joy alternated, say with the ticking of a clock, here we should not have the characteristic formation of the pattern of sorrow or of the pattern of joy (Wittgenstein, *Philosophical Investigations*, II, i).

The phases through which a sensation passes may coincide with the phases which are characteristic of an emotion. By a fluke, Jack may have a bout of rheumatism which starts at the same time as, lasts as long as, and waxes and wanes in time with, a love-affair of Jill's. But any pattern is accidental to a sensation, while some pattern is essential to an emotion. "Is it possible to fall in love at first sight?" is not the same sort of question as "Is it possible to be seasick as soon as one steps afloat?"

The most important difference between a sensation and an emotion is that emotions, unlike sensations, are essentially directed to objects. It is possible to be hungry without being hungry for anything in particular, as it is not possible to be ashamed without being ashamed of anything in particular. It is possible to be in pain without knowing what is hurting one, as it is not possible to be delighted without knowing what is delighting one. It is not in general possible to ascribe a piece of behaviour or a sensation to a particular emotional state without at the same time ascribing an object to the emotion. If a man runs past me I can say nothing about his emotions unless I know whether he is running away from A or running towards B; no flutterings of the heart or meltings of the bowels could tell me I was in love without telling me with whom.

But are there not objectless emotions, such as pointless depression and undirected fears? And does not their existence show that the connection between an emotion and its object is purely contingent? There are indeed such emotions, though some emotions often described as objectless are not so in fact. We are often unaccountably depressed, on days when for no reason everything seems black; but pointless depression is not objectless depression, and the objects of depression are the things which seem black. A phobia, again, is not a fear without an object, but a fear without an adequate object; the agoraphobe may have no reason for being afraid, but he is afraid *of* something, namely open spaces.

Still, there are cases where we are afraid, but afraid of nothing, or of something, but we know not what.[1] Perhaps we awake in the morning with a sinking feeling, and a loose and general sense of dread; only later do we remember a dangerous task to be performed. Or a man may be paralysed by a conviction of impending doom, though he can give no account of what he dreads. In the first case, the early morning experience may be described in physical terms or emotional terms. If the former, then it is possible that it may later turn out to be some emotion other than fear (e.g. if the thought later occurring is of some disastrous mistake already made). If the latter, then the emotional terms derive their appropriateness from the fact that the physical sensation was later followed by the anticipation of ill. To be sure, the words "I am afraid" may well have come into the subject's mind *before* the thought of the future danger; but if such words occurred to him regularly divorced from all such context, they would gradually lose their meaning. In the case of the neurotic fear, the neurosis is described

[1] Freud preferred the second formulation of the definition of *Angst* (*Collected Works*, XVIII, 12). On the relationship between the two formulations see Wittgenstein, *The Blue Book*, 22ff. "*Angst*" is often used to refer to cases of a different type, where the subject *does* assign an object to his fears, but an inadequate one, which a psychoanalyst regards as a symbol for some other, hidden object.

as "fear" partly because the verbal behaviour of the neurotic echoes the utterances of those who have ordinary object-directed fears, partly because immobilisation is part of the behaviour pattern of nonneurotic fears of certain objects. The use of the word "fear" in such cases is therefore dependent upon its use in cases where fear has an object.

Despite such cases, therefore, the connection between emotions and their objects is not a contingent one. The philosophers considered earlier consistently neglected this fact. The pattern of "act and object" was present in their accounts but the active verb was "perceive" and the object was the emotion itself presented to inner perception. And *this* object was not related, except causally, to any object of its own; for an emotion was private and mental and its object (frequently) public and physical.

I denied that there could be a private object of this kind, on the grounds that sense could not be attached to any word purporting to refer to such an object. To avoid misunderstanding, it is perhaps necessary to explain in what sense emotions *are* private, and how the names for the emotions *are* learnt.

Emotions, like other mental states, may be manifested or kept to oneself. In denying that they are essentially private states, one is not denying the possibility of keeping them secret. One is rather denying the possibility that there might be a race of men who felt all the emotions that we feel, but never manifested them publicly by word or deed. Only beings who are capable of manifesting a particular emotion are capable of experiencing it. In particular, those emotions which can be manifested only by the use of language (e.g. remorse for a crime committed long ago, or fear about the distant future) can be experienced only by language-using beings.

But though one *can* experience an emotion only if one *can* manifest it, it does not follow that one *does* experience an emotion only if one *does* manifest it. There are indeed some emotions for which the stronger thesis holds: a man cannot be in a violent rage or extreme anguish if his countenance is serene and he talks composedly about indifferent topics. One of the criteria of intensity for such emotions is that they should be incapable of being concealed; as we talk of overmastering anger and overpowering grief. On the other hand, it is clearly possible to be afraid of something, or in love with someone, without telling anybody about it. Is it also possible to experience these emotions without betraying them *in any way*?

There seems to be a difference here between emotions and other states of mind, such as beliefs. It is quite clearly possible to have a belief and to go to one's grave without telling anyone about it and without doing anything about it. We are constantly noticing odd facts and collecting scraps of information (e.g. that there is a cloud the shape of a pig above the church, or that there are two misprints in *The Times* fourth leader) which are too trivial either to affect our behaviour or to be worth passing on. But beliefs, by themselves, do not lead to action; whereas desires and emotions do. The possibility of a completely unexpressed belief does not, therefore, by itself show the possibility of a completely unexpressed emotion.

Earlier, we made a distinction between emotion as motive and emotion as feeling. It is clear that for an emotion to function as a motive the person whose emotion it is must *do* something; otherwise there will be nothing for the emotion-motive to explain. If John is in love with Mary, then he must in some way or other conduct his life differently from a man who is not in love with Mary. But there seems no reason to think that what is done in such cases must always be something public; perhaps the only upshot of a man's love for a woman may be that he thinks a lot about her. To be sure, in that case, we shall want some explanation why his love goes no further; but such explanations are frequently to be found—perhaps Mary is already happily married.

Where there are feelings of emotion which are not acted on, there will still be both sensations and thoughts. The thoughts may be private as any other thoughts may; what of the sensations? Sensations too, it seems, may be private; one may feel hungry, and yet tell no one of this, and eat no more and no sooner than one does on days when one does not feel hungry. Still, even if there are no marks of hunger in the face, there are bodily states and changes characteristic of hunger which could be detected with the appropriate apparatus. Similarly, might not some Big Brother, armed with a battery of technical devices, put himself into a position to observe all our most secret moods and passions? Only if he could observe also the thoughts; for it is not in general possible to identify an emotion without identifying also its object; and where, *ex hypothesi*, an emotion takes the form of a feeling which is not acted upon, the connection with the object can be made only by the thoughts which surround the sensation. The non-contingent connection between emotions and behaviour, and between sensations and behaviour, does not *entail* any impossibility of keeping both emotions and sensations secret. If it is a fact that a man's every thought and every feeling is capable of being read in his brain-traces and in his blood chemistry, as it can be read in his spoken words and his visible gestures, then this is a contingent fact, and yet to be discovered.

In some cases, the manifestation of an emotion is the result of a decision; in other cases, it is the non-manifestation of the emotion which is the result of decision and perhaps effort. Thus, we may have to bring ourselves to the sticking-point after long preparation in order to reveal our love or confess our shame; on the other hand, it may call for constantly renewed effort to stop our anger breaking out, perpetual vigilance to prevent our fear from becoming obvious.

It is possible, then, for feelings of emotion to be kept to oneself, and, in that sense, to be private. But it does not follow from the fact that some emotions are private events that all emotions could be private events. "What sometimes happens could always happen" is a fallacy. It is the case that some money is forged; it could not be the case that all money was forged. Some men are taller than average; it could not be the case that all men were taller than average.

The reason why it is not possible that all emotions should be concealed emotions is that if they were, the meaning of emotion-words could never be learnt. The empiricist picture was that one learned the name of a particular emotion by observing in one's own experience the occurrence of a sample of that emotion.

On this view, one would never know that the experience one called by the name of a particular emotion was the same as that which others called by the same name.

In place of this theory, Wittgenstein offered, in the case of sensations, a different view of the learning of meanings. Words are connected with the primitive and natural expressions of sensation and used in their place. A child has hurt himself and he cries; and then adults talk to him and teach him exclamations and later sentences. Thus they teach the child new pain-behaviour (*Philosophical Investigations*, I, 244).

We can apply this to the learning of emotion-words. The child runs to his mother, and she says: "Don't be frightened!"; or he trembles, and she asks: "What are you afraid of?" But we meet a difficulty here. We have all along insisted that there is no pattern of behaviour common to every manifestation of a single emotion *no matter what its object*. We cannot therefore simply say that emotion-words are taught as a replacement of emotional behaviour; for no matter how we describe a piece of behaviour, it will only be *emotional* behaviour if it occurs in the appropriate circumstances. If the child cries, for example, we shall know whether to call this pain-behaviour or emotional behaviour only if we know whether he is crying because, say, he has bumped his head or because he has been left alone. The language of the emotions must therefore be taught in connection not only with emotional behaviour, but above all in connection with objects of emotion. It is in connection with fearful objects, pleasant tastes, and annoying circumstances that the child learns the verbal expression of fear, pleasure, and anger.

The concept of each emotion is linked with non-emotional concepts in three ways. The concept, for example, of *fear* stands on three struts:

    (*a*) fearful circumstances
    (*b*) symptoms of fear
    (*c*) action taken to avoid what is feared.

Just as the verbal expression of fear must be learnt in the context of these factors, so it can be understood only in the context of one or other of them. In the standard case, which is both the paradigm for learning and the most easily intelligible, all three factors will be present. The man-eating lion advances roaring; the defenceless planter screams, pales, and takes to his heels. His later report "I was terrified" is as fully intelligible as such a report can be. But the verbal expression of fear remains intelligible when one, or even two, of these factors is absent but the third remains. Many people show symptoms of fear and take avoiding action in circumstances which are not dangerous and not frightening to most people; fears of this type are so common that we have names for some of them ("agoraphobia", "claustrophobia", and so on) and words for the liability or proneness to such fears ("timorousness", "cowardice", etc.). Again, there is the case where in fearful circumstances the victim shows manifest symptoms of fear but takes no action to avoid impending danger: as a man may be rooted to the spot with terror, or watch the uncoiling cobra with helpless fascination. These cases also are so very frequent that we take a certain type of inaction as being itself a symptom of fear. And then there are the many cases where there are fearful circumstances, and where there is avoiding action, but where there are no symptoms of fear. The precautions which we take against diseases are motivated by fear of serious enough danger yet in the majority of cases the taking of precautions—e.g. by vaccination—is a cold-blooded affair, quite unaccompanied by quakings, blanchings, gooseflesh or hysterical screams.

In the cases we have so far considered, two of the three listed features have been present to render intelligible any verbal expression of fear which occurs in their context. There are also cases where only one of the props remains to support the claim to be afraid. The soldier going into battle may stiffen his upper lip and repress any desire to run away; symptoms and avoiding action are absent, but the circumstances alone render quite intelligible any later confession of fear. Again, a man may make a policy of never travelling in trains, at whatever cost in inconvenience. Because he never goes on a train, we never have a chance to catch him trembling, or to measure his PGR on a train-journey; still, his perseverance in his policy is itself enough to render intelligible his coy admission "I am afraid of trains".

But if all three features are missing, there seems to be no foothold at all for fear. If a man says that he feels frightened, but shows no sign of fear and takes no particular action, we will understand and may believe him; but not if, when asked why, he says "because it is five to three". We may still cast about for an explanation: does he believe that the last judgement is going to take place at three, or something of the kind? If he then replies "Oh, for no particular reason; I feel like this at five to three every day"—would we not wonder why, whatever he felt, he called his feeling "fear"? But perhaps even in this case the word need not have lost all meaning. Provided only that the man normally uses the word "fear" as we all do, in connection with the three broad conditions of intelligibility sketched above, then it remains, after all, an interesting fact that it was the word "fear", and not, say "sadness" which sprang spontaneously to his mind to describe his feelings. We might say that the absolute minimum which is required in order that a man's state of mind should be rightly called "fear" is that it should be a state of mind in which the verbal expression of fear comes naturally to a man who has learnt and customarily exercises the normal use of the word "fear". But if a man regularly used the word in the way described above, then all that we could say was that he did not understand what it meant; and of any word in an unknown language which was regularly so used, we could say for certain that it did not mean fear.

In such a case as the one considered, the *only* outward sign with which the man's inner state is non-contingently connected is precisely the word "fear"; which is merely another way of saying that his use of the word is here the only criterion which we have for calling his feeling "fear". We have here come as close as it is possible to get to a genuine internal impression: for an internal impression was an inner event connected only contingently with everything else in its owner's behaviour except his use of a name. The attempt to explain the life of the mind in terms of internal impressions was therefore tantamount to taking the oddest possible emotions, and the most freakish possible uses of words, as the standard cases by which to explain all others.

It is necessary to mention two points which, for simplicity's sake, were slurred over in the discussion of the last few paragraphs. I have been purporting to give an account of the way in which the concept of an emotion was linked with non-emotional concepts. But in describing the props on which the concept of "fear" stood I used expressions such as "fearful circumstances", "symptoms of fear" so that it may have looked as if my account was circular. I used such expressions merely for brevity; they could be replaced, without loss of explanatory force, by expressions which make no mention of fear. "Fearful circumstances", for instance, could be replaced by "dangerous circumstances"; the concept of *danger* does not involve reference to the emotions, since we can speak of danger to plants or artefacts, which cannot have emotions. The symptoms of fear could be given a purely physical description; many of them, such as fluctuations of breathing-rate, are shared with other emotions and might be produced by purely physical causes. Avoiding action can be explained purely in terms of intention, without reference to emotion.

Secondly, again for simplicity's sake, I have written as if the verbal expression of fear had to be tied on to non-verbal behaviour and circumstance without the possibility of its being linked through other verbal behaviour. But clearly there are verbal signs of fear other than the explicit utterance of fear; the action taken to avoid a fearful object might be purely verbal action (e.g. ordering someone out of the way); while the danger to be avoided might be something which only a language-user could appreciate, such as the danger of insulting somebody important. A man's avowal of fear may be made intelligible in very complex ways by its connection with other parts of his verbal behaviour. So, for completeness, we should add to our three sufficient conditions of intelligibility a fourth: the speaker's use of connected and similar concepts.

Descartes, as we have seen, made no systematic distinction between the cause of an emotion and its object; Hume did, but for him the object was connected with the emotion no less contingently than the cause. For both these philosophers, to say that a child is afraid of the fire is to say that the mental event which is his fear is the effect of which the fire he now sees is the cause. Wittgenstein writes:

We should distinguish between the object of fear and the cause of fear.

Thus a face which inspires fear or delight (the object of fear or delight) is not on that account its cause, but—one might say—its target.

When the burnt child dreads the fire, the object of his fear is the fire which he is here and now afraid of; but his present fear is the effect of his past experience (*Philosophical Investigations*, I, 476).

There are many cases in which it is very natural to think of the object of an emotion as its cause. "I was frightened by the face at the window", "I was angry because he burst in without knocking", "Her behaviour made me most embarrassed" all assign objects to emotions by means of forms of descriptions that are ostensibly causal. Sometimes, also, we give genuinely causal accounts of emotions without specifying any objects for them: "I was irritable because I was hungry", "I felt completely serene because I was

71

drunk". There may well be, we feel, physical processes which link the events in the eyes, when the startling face is seen, to the bodily events which express the startle; and so in the other situations.

There are, on the other hand, cases where the object of an emotion is quite clearly distinct from its cause. This is most obviously so in the case of forward-looking emotions, such as hope, dread, and excited anticipation, where the object of the emotion is something which is as yet in the future and therefore cannot be the cause of the emotion which belongs to the present. "I dread the next war" does not report the occurrence in me of an event caused by the next war, nor can "I hope Eclipse will win" be replaced by "I am hopeful, because Eclipse will win". There are other cases, too, where an emotion is not the one which would naturally be caused by its object: when the hero scorns the danger, there is no temptation to think that there is a causal chain which begins with the danger and ends with the scorn, and when the judge hardens his heart against the widow his hardening is not the effect of her tears.

Descartes himself noticed these last cases, and gave an *ad hoc* explanation of them. [1] In the other cases a Cartesian might say that dread of the next war, for example, is caused not by the next war, but by the image of the next war. But this is already to admit that the object of an emotion differs from its cause: to be afraid of an image is not the same as to be afraid of a war, and even if we accept the idea of a causal relation between the image and the dread, the dread is not dread *of* the image.

[1] *Les Passions de l'Ame*, 173.

But how could one be certain that the dread was caused by the image, and not by one of the many other things which may be happening at the same time? If the relation between an emotion and its object were one of effect to cause, then it would be only by induction and tentative hypothesis that one knew on any particular occasion *what* one was afraid of or excited about. But this is sometimes obviously untrue. If I feel great happiness and relief because my wife unexpectedly recovers from a mortal illness, I do not first discover that I feel happy and relieved, and then draw the conclusion that this feeling is caused by my wife's recovery (e.g. on the grounds that I have observed that whenever she so recovers I have just *this* feeling). There are indeed cases where one feels depressed for no particular reason, or is made uncomfortable by a vague feeling of apprehension. But there are not cases where one is in doubt which of two disasters one is afraid of, or when one knows that one is expecting bad news, but is not yet sure what the bad news is that one is expecting.

Causes are assigned to particular emotions, and objects to unspecified emotions; this is because emotions are specified by their objects. That is to say: if someone betrays the marks of some emotion (as fear or embarrassment) we may seek to find the object of his emotion, by asking "what are you afraid of?" or "what is embarrassing you?" Having learnt the object of the emotion, we may then go on to ask such questions as "but why are you afraid of the dark?" or "but why do bawdy jokes embarrass you?"; and the answer to these questions may, though it need not, assign a cause for the emotions thus specified. In such cases,

F   73

we are seeking a cause for a general tendency to experience certain emotions in certain situations, or at
certain objects. In other cases we may seek a cause
for a particular emotion at a particular time: as
when we ask why the manager has been so irritated
this morning at small things (object) and learn that it
is because he is suffering from dyspepsia (cause).
Causes are sought for emotions-regarding-particular-
objects, not for emotions *simpliciter*: we look for the
causes of a man's fear of mice, or dislike of strawberries; we do not look for the causes of his fear, or
his dislike: for this would be to ask the question "why
does he have fears?" or "why does he have dislikes?" to
which the only answer seems to be: because he is a
human being.

There are many locutions of quite distinct structures
to express the relations between an emotion and its
object. Thus, we may say "I was angry with him,
not because of what he said, but because of the way he
spoke" or "I was angry at his way of speaking, not at
what he said" or "It was the way he spoke, not what
he said, that made me angry". The difference between
these sentences is purely of idiom, not at all of meaning. Yet the apparent logical structure of each is
different from that of the others. Contrast with these
the sentence "I was angry with him, because I was
hungry". Here, the apparent logical structure is
similar to that of the first of the sentences above: the
real logical structure is quite different, for the sentence
does not admit of translation into the other forms. "I
was angry at my being hungry" means something
quite different from "I was angry because I was
hungry". In the one case we have the object, in the

other the cause, of an emotion. The distinction between the cause and the object of an emotion is thus
most easily made out by reference to the knowledge or
beliefs of the subject. Faced with any sentence
describing the occurrence of an emotion, of the form
"A ϕd because p", we must ask whether it is a necessary condition of the truth of this sentence that A
should know or believe that p. If so, then the sentence
contains an allusion to the object of the emotion; if
not, to its cause. Thus, to take the previous example,
I cannot be angry because of the way a man speaks
if I do not notice the way he speaks; but I may well
be angry because I am hungry without realizing that
I am hungry. Similarly, "I feel elated because I have
just been complimented" suggests that I believe that
I have just been complimented; whereas I may feel
elated because I am drunk, though I may not know
that I am drunk and may boldly contradict anyone
who suggests that I am. My being complimented is the
object, and my being drunk a cause, of my elation.

It may happen on occasion that a single state of
affairs is both object and cause of the same emotion;
for while a man *need* not know the cause of his
emotions, he *may* do so. Thus, when a man feels
depressed because of his failing health, his debility is
both the object and the cause of his feeling of depression.

CHAPTER FOUR

MOTIVES

THE concepts of the several emotions are employed not only in the description of feelings but also in the explanation of actions. We feel fear, and also act out of fear; love is not only a sentiment, but also a motive of action. We have already had several occasions to distinguish between emotions as feelings, and emotions as motives. It is time to discuss the concept of "motive" in a more systematic way.

Professor Ryle, in discussing emotions, distinguishes between inclinations, moods, agitations and feelings. "Motive" for him is a synonym for "inclination"; and as examples of inclinations he suggests vanity, kindliness, avarice, patriotism, laziness, interest in symbolic logic, a determination to become a bishop, and keenness on gardening. He distinguishes between inclinations of this kind and feelings such as a throb of compassion, a glow of pride, and a sinking sensation of despair.

Ryle is anxious to combat a particular view of the relationship between feelings and motives. He is concerned above all to demonstrate that to say that a man acted out of a certain motive is not to say that his action was preceded and caused by the occurrence of the corresponding feeling. His arguments to this effect are well known and for the most part wholly convincing. I shall not, therefore, discuss them.

His positive account of what it is to act from a motive, however, seems open to objection. He presents the issue as follows:

The statement "He boasted from vanity" ought, on one view, to be construed as saying that "he boasted and the cause of his boasting was the occurrence in him of a particular feeling or impulse of vanity". On the other view [which Ryle adopts] it is to be construed as saying "he boasted on meeting the stranger and his doing so satisfied the law-like proposition that whenever he finds a chance of securing the admiration and envy of others, he does whatever he thinks will produce this admiration and envy" (*The Concept of Mind*, 89).

To say [that a man did something from a certain motive] is to say that this action, done in its particular circumstances, was just the sort of thing that that was an inclination to do. It is to say "he *would* do that" (92).

One may well feel that Ryle has not here exhausted the possible accounts of the nature of motives. It seems possible to agree with Ryle in rejecting the causal-influence-of-feelings theory without agreeing with him in accepting the law-like-generalization theory. Miss Anscombe has pointed out that the second theory seems to lead to the conclusion that one cannot act out of a motive on one occasion only (*Intention*, 21). But it seems possible to act out of vanity once in a while, out of impatience without being an impatient man, and out of remorse without being chronically remorseful.

Ryle is correct in saying that to act out of vanity is

to do the sort of thing that a vain man would do; but such a truism, if offered as an account of vanity, is quite innocent of explanatory force. If I claim to have discovered a new emotion of wubbliness, I cannot communicate its nature by saying that it is that emotion which impels me to do all and only those actions which a wubbly man would do. Ryle's account does indeed contain an explanatory element; but the explanation is contained not in the generalization, but in the description of the action which is generalized. In the case in point, it is already established that the man boasted from vanity if we can say that his only aim was to secure the admiration and envy of the stranger. In this case (whatever may be true in other cases) once we know the man's intention we can ascribe to him a motive; it does not matter whether he habitually acts with such an intention. It is possible that Ryle would give an account of intention similar to that which he gives of motives: namely, that a man can act with a certain intention only if he habitually so acts. But this is already much less plausible. For while a motive is very often assigned by means of a word, such as "vanity", which can also stand for an abiding trait of character, the characteristic form of an assignation of intention is a reference to a particular state of affairs which the agent desires to realize.

There is in any case something odd about Ryle's example. "He boasted out of vanity" adds little to "He boasted"; for to boast is precisely to make vain remarks about oneself. Boasting is a sign of vanity, and, in general, emotions are not called in to explain their own obvious manifestations. If a man laughs genuinely and heartily, we do not need to explain that he does so because he is amused. Reference to emotion is appropriate in the explanation of actions which are not an immediate and characteristic manifestation of such an emotion; as when we say that somebody made a foolish mistake, or did a job badly, because he was in love, or was suffering some secret sorrow. Where symptoms are shared by various emotions, then it is appropriate to explain the symptoms by reference to the particular emotion in question: the tears, we may explain, were tears of joy and not of sorrow.

It is ironic that Ryle, having attacked the 'impulse' theory of motives for wrongly regarding explanation by motives as a type of causal explanation, should himself offer a theory which is, on his own view of causation, no less causal. For if to offer X as a causal explanation of Y is roughly to say that whenever X then Y, then Ryle's explication of "he boasted from vanity" as "whenever an opportunity for boasting arrives, he takes it" construes "he boasted from vanity" as a causal statement. His theory differs from the one he rejects only in that it offers public circumstances, instead of private impulses, as the cause of the boasting.

Ryle's account of the relation between motives and feelings seems no more satisfactory than his account of the relation between motives and actions. He asserts, indeed, that feelings are not intrinsically connected with motives, but rather with agitations, such as suspense and horror. However, many of the examples which he gives of feelings—such as glows of pride, tugs of commiseration, and throbs of compassion—are feelings *of* things which Ryle rightly lists among possible motives. Fundamentally, his account of such feelings runs as follows. A report such as "I feel a twinge of remorse" embodies a hypothesis which may be mistaken. When we are "attaching a feeling to an emotional condition, we are applying a causal hypothesis". Remorse, in other words, is related to twinges of remorse as cause to effect (*Op. cit.*, 105).

Now if this cause-effect story is to be the true one, it must be possible to identify the effect independently of the cause. We must be able to say "this is the same kind of twinge as I felt yesterday", without making any appeal to what the twinge is a twinge *of* as a criterion of identity. Otherwise there is no room for an inductive hypothesis based on an observed correlation. It must be possible, on Ryle's view, to know that one has a tug, but not to know that it is a tug of commiseration. The meaning of the word "tug" in this context must be learnt quite independently of the meaning of the word "commiseration".

It seems to be the case, however, that we know what "tug" means in this context only because we are familiar with the use of "commiseration". It is the same with "twinges", "flutters", "throbs", "glows", "qualms", and all the other words in Ryle's rich vocabulary of feeling-words. It is because we know about the various states which these feelings are feelings of that we can see and applaud the appropriateness of the words which Ryle employs for the feelings themselves.

Ryle does not suggest how the meaning of a word like "twinge" might be learnt. It does not seem as if it could be learnt in connection with any non-verbal behaviour characteristic of twinges; since, for Ryle, a twinge may be a perfectly good twinge whether it is

connected with the behaviour characteristic of toothache or the behaviour characteristic of remorse. It
looks as if one is supposed to learn the meaning of
"twinge" merely by having twinges, rather as empiricist philosophers thought that one could learn
the meaning of the word "red" merely by having red
sense-data. Altogether, Ryle seems to have imperfectly
exorcised the ghost of Locke. Internal impressions
were firmly banished in his account of motives; they
turn up again in the guise of feelings. It is noteworthy
that in this passage Ryle treats the first-person usage
as standard, in marked contrast to his procedure
elsewhere. Normally he correctly starts from the
question "How do I know that another man has such
and such a motive, or skill, or state of mind?" Here
he takes as his paradigm the question: "How do I
know what *my* feelings are feelings of?"

Ryle gives two arguments for his thesis.

First, he draws an analogy between bodily sensations and feelings. We learn to locate sensations, he
says, and to give their crude physiological diagnoses
from a rule-of-thumb experimental process rein-
forced by lessons from others. The pain is in the finger
in which I see the needle; it is in that finger by the
sucking of which alone the pain is alleviated. Similarly,
he suggests, when we report feelings *of* something, we
are essaying a diagnosis of the feeling on the basis of
rough and ready experimentation.

The analogy between feelings and sensation is
genuine enough and has already been discussed. The
weakness of Ryle's argument is in his description of
the analogate. Localizing one's pain, in the sense of
being able to say where one's pain is, is indeed a skill

which has to be taught. But it is not as if the child is first taught what "the pain is in my little finger" *means*, and then, by a separate process, learns the circumstances under which this is *true*. He does not first attach a sense to "the pain is in my little finger" and then establish empirical laws such as "whenever I have a pain which is alleviated by sucking my little finger, I have independently observed that the pain has been in my little finger". If the baby can independently observe that the pain is in his little finger, why does he need to go through the roundabout process of correlation? If he cannot, then how can a merely causal correlation between the cessation of pain and the sucking of the finger show that the pain was really in the little finger? Why should there not be a causal correlation between sucking the little finger and the cessation of pain in the big toe, as there is a causal correlation between defecation and the cessation of headaches? "The pain is in that finger in which I see the pin" is more like a definition than a correlation. The analogy between pain and feelings, therefore, supplies no ground for saying that remorse is related to twinges of remorse as cause to effect.[1]

Ryle's second argument is based on the possibility

---

[1] "The pain is in the finger in which I see the pin" is not quite a definition, for it gives only one criterion for localizing pain. Pain is localized by two criteria (a) the place of the injury (b) the place spontaneously attended to by sucking, caressing, pointing, etc. The two criteria may conflict, as when a man points out to a dentist a tooth other than that decayed. Where a conflict occurs we say sometimes that the patient is mistaken (as in the toothache case), sometimes that the pain is located, oddly, elsewhere than the injury (as is the case of referred pain). But unless the two criteria in general coincided in their results we could not have the concept of *pain* which we have.

of being mistaken about what one's feeling is a feeling *of*. One may diagnose as a twinge of remorse what is really a twinge of fear, or ascribe to excitement fluttering sensations caused by oversmoking. Therefore, a report of a twinge of remorse or of a flutter of excitement embodies a fallible hypothesis about the cause of the twinge or the flutter.

Such cases do occur, but they do not prove Ryle's conclusion from his premises. For Ryle, to say that a feeling is caused by a certain emotion is to say no more than that it is the sort of feeling which is had by people who are in the emotional state in question. But on this view, the hypothesis that a flutter was caused by oversmoking by no means excludes the hypothesis that it was due to excitement. For to say that it was due to excitement is merely to say that it was the sort of feeling that excited people have; and this it may be—indeed must be, if there is to be a possibility of mistaking it for a feeling of excitement—even though caused by oversmoking.

Just as we can often describe a face straight off as angry, without being able to give any other description of the play of the features, so we can often describe our feelings as remorseful or excited without being able to give any description of them which would be free of emotional overtones. It cannot therefore be in general true that to ascribe a feeling to a particular emotion is to make a hypothesis about its cause. "This feeling is due to dyspepsia, not anxiety" is the logical product of two statements, one of which is a causal hypothesis and the other something different. We have already discussed a sense in which reports of emotions may be mistaken; but when they are mistakes, they are not erroneous causal hypotheses. A feeling of anxiety is non-contingently related to the alarming circumstances which give rise to it; the relation between dyspepsia and its cause is purely contingent. A particular sensation in the stomach could be my only indication that I had indigestion; it could not be my only indication that I was anxious.

Miss Anscombe, in *Intention*, offers an account of motives which differs from Ryle's. She divides motives into three classes: (*a*) those which are equivalent to intentions; (*b*) backward-looking motives, such as remorse and gratitude, which assign something in the past or present as the ground of an action; (*c*) interpretative motives, such as friendship and curiosity, which place an action in a certain light.

Miss Anscombe is at pains to distinguish between backward-looking motives and "mental causes". (An example of an assignation of a mental cause is the sentence "The martial music excites me, which is why I walk up and down".) Motives differ from mental causes in being bound up with good and ill.

If an action has to be thought of by the agent as doing good or harm of some sort, and the thing in the past [which is mentioned as the ground for acting] as good or bad, in order for the thing in the past to be the reason for the action, then this reason shews not a mental cause but a motive. ... E.g. if I am grateful to someone, it is because he has done me some good, or at least I think he has, and I cannot show gratitude by something that I intend to harm him (*Intention*, 22, 21).

Miss Anscombe's distinctions are valuable, but her account seems to leave unanswered the question: how do motives *explain* actions? No less than Ryle, she rejects the suggestion that motivated actions are causally determined by preceding feelings. She writes, for example, "If we wanted to explain, e.g., revenge, we should say it was harming someone because he had done one some harm; we should not need to add to this a description of the feelings prompting the action or the thought that had gone with it." Perhaps so: but one of the things we want to know is the force of the *because* here, and this Miss Anscombe does not explain. Ryle's account, mistaken though it was, did at least attempt to bring motivation under one familiar concept of explanation.

The difficulty in giving an account of the concept of *motive* arises partly from a vagueness in the concept itself. What words count as motive-words? Several answers, equally plausible, suggest themselves. A motive-word, we may say, is a word which is an appropriate completion of the following sentence frames: "He acted out of ... ", " ... made him do such-and-such", "He did such-and-such because he was ... ", "His motive in doing such-and-such was ... ". Unfortunately, the use of these sentence-frames to define motives produces four lists of words which by no means coincide.

There are indeed many names of motives which can complete any of the four frames. We may say of Macbeth that he murdered Duncan out of ambition, that it was his ambition which made him commit the crime, that he killed his guest because he was ambitious, and that his motive in so doing was ambition. Vanity, patriotism, despair, greed, gratitude, politeness, desire and fear, like ambition, count as motives by all of the four criteria. But each criterion lets in some things which by the other criteria we would be disinclined to count as a motive. Thus, one can make a mistake out of impatience, drop a catch out of carelessness, or stay in bed out of idleness; but we would not say that impatience was a motive for making a mistake, or that carelessness motivated one's dropping of a catch, or that one's motive for staying in bed was idleness. Again, a market researcher may decide that it is the red silver paper which makes the public buy Blogg's biscuits rather than Snogg's; but red silver paper is not their motive in buying anybody's biscuits. A man might fight well because he is courageous, a woman may resist advances because she is chaste, and a child may get a sum wrong because he is distracted, but one does not act out of courage or out of chastity, and distraction is not a motive. Paradoxically, even the phrase "his motive in doing such and such was ..." frequently serves to introduce an infinitive, which would more naturally be said to refer to an intention than to a motive.

Motives and intentions are clearly connected, and it is not easy to make any sharp distinction between them. It is sometimes said that when a reason for action refers to something prior, or contemporaneous with the action, it is a motive; when it refers to some future state of affairs to be brought about by the action, then it is an intention. This is a useful distinction, even if it does not accord with usage; yet it is easily made to seem trivial. For any explanation of an action by an intention ("He did it to ϕ") seems to be easy to recast into what, on this criterion, is an explanation by motive (e.g. "He did it out of a desire to ϕ"). And there are indeed many cases where we can say: Tell me a man's intentions and I will tell you his motives; tell me his motives and I will tell you his intentions.

The notion of *motive* is much more sophisticated than that of *intention*. It has been said, I do not know with what truth, that no other language has a word corresponding totally to the English word "motive"; though, of course, other languages have forms of expression corresponding to our "acting out of . . ." and it is usually possible to find translations for the names of particular motives. It is possible to write long and detailed historical narrative without bringing in any reference to motives to explain actions;[1] while no narrative is recognizable as a description of human behaviour unless it makes continual reference to intentions and intentional actions. It is possible to act from a motive without possessing any concept of the motive from which one acts; as it is not possible to act for a purpose without a concept of the purpose for which one acts. Caesar's style in the *De Bello Gallico* can be clearly seen to have been motivated by lifemanship; but he cannot have possessed a concept which was invented only in our own time. On the other hand, one frequently sees men who know no Greek being stirred to action by *megalopsychia*.

One cannot have an intention for a motive, but one may have a motive for an intention, like Macbeth, who had no spur to prick the sides of his intent but

---

[1] If anyone finds this surprising, let him read through the first six chapters of St Mark's Gospel. No explanation by motive ever appears; the names of the emotions are used purely descriptively, as in "he looked round angrily".

vaulting ambition. This is because both motives and intentions admit of ascription only to voluntary actions: and intending to do something is itself a voluntary action, whereas having a particular motive is not.[1] For this reason, it is incorrect to say that whenever what a man does is explained by reference to an emotional state a motive is assigned; one may make a slip because one is in love, but love is not the motive of one's slip, because making a slip is not a fully voluntary action.

Someone who realizes how difficult it is either to distinguish between motive and intention or to identify one with the other may be tempted to explore here a line of thought familiar in other branches of philosophy. He might be struck by the fact that Ryle's list of motives is composed almost entirely of the names of virtues and vices; he mentions vanity, kindliness, avarice, patriotism, laziness, philanthropy and consideration for others. Virtues and vices are clearly connected with praise and blame. Might it not be then, that when we ascribe a motive, all we are doing over and above assigning an intention is to praise or blame the intention so assigned?[2] Thus, to say that a

[1] Miss Anscombe writes: "it is a mistake to think one cannot choose whether to act from a motive. Plato saying to a slave 'I should beat you if I were not angry' would be a case" (*Intention*, 22). This is misleading. It is true that one may be motivated to an action, and, knowing this, choose not to act; as an M.P. may declare his interest and abstain from debate. But, having chosen, for whatever reason, to do a certain action, there is then no room for a further choice to settle what motive one will act from, except by choosing to perform some second action which may set the first in an altered context.

[2] We cannot, of course, say that it is to praise or blame *the action*. To be sure, one takes a more charitable view of an action if one attributes it to patriotism than if one attributes it to cupidity; but it is notorious that bad actions may be done with good motives.

man told a story out of vanity will be to say that he
told it in order to arouse the admiration of his hearers,
and to condemn him for wanting to do this. To say
that a man ate ten pork pies out of gluttony will be to
say that he ate them purely for pleasure, and to express our disapproval of this. Support for this view of
motives as essentially evaluative may come from a
consideration of those cases where two people may
agree on a man's intentions in acting in a certain way,
and disagree about his motives. Peter and Paul may
agree that a certain journalist writes his reports in
such a manner as to show his own country in the best
light possible; Peter may attribute his action to
patriotism, and Paul to jingoism. It may be common
ground that an evangelist devotes his life to making
proselytes, and yet a matter for discussion whether he
does so out of bigotry or out of zeal. So, we may be
tempted to think of the distinction between motives
and intentions as a further example of the much-
canvassed distinction between evaluative and descriptive language.

There are strong objections on general grounds to
theories of the type we have just exemplified.[1] For
our purposes, it is enough to note that there are many
motives which the theory does not fit at all. It cannot
explain those cases where the motive assigned is not a
virtue or a vice but, e.g., friendship, admiration,
curiosity, anxiety or nostalgia. Nor can it explain
those cases where to assign a motive is not, or not
obviously, to assign an intention at all; as with
revenge, gratitude, and remorse.

[1] Cf. Geach, "Ascriptivism", *The Philosophical Review*, April
1960, 222–223.

If we are to give a general account of motives, we must start elsewhere. There are many backward-looking reasons for action which are not the sort of reasons which spring to mind when we talk of motives. Consider the following sentences: "I'm coming indoors because it's cold", "I gave him £5 because I owed it to him", "He bought a new suit because his old one was too small", "They sacked him because he was drunk on his job". These sentences have obviously much in common with "I killed him because he killed my father". Yet there is no motive-word which occurs naturally in connection with the first four sentences as "revenge" does with the fifth.

Each of these sentences exemplifies, in a more or less complex way, a single fundamental pattern of description and explanation of human behaviour. Very often, what happens when a human being performs an action may be described as follows. First, there exists a state of affairs of which the agent disapproves; then the agent does something; after his action there exists, in place of the original state of affairs, a different state of affairs of which he approves. A particular and common form of this scheme applies when each of the states of affairs in question consists of the possession of a property by the agent himself. Thus, where ". . . is P" and ". . . is Q" are incompatible predicates, first A is P and does not want to be; then A acts; then A is Q and is content to be.[1] This pattern has numerous simple exemplifications: as when a man, being cold, goes to the fire and gets warm; or, being dirty, washes himself clean.

[1] In the limiting cases, "P" will be "not Q", or "Q" will be "not P".

Wherever this scheme of description of action applies, there will be room for three main types of explanation of action. An action may be explained by reference to the unwanted state of affairs which preceded it, or by reference to the wanted state of affairs which was, or was expected to be, its upshot, or by some form of explanation which alludes to both of these together. Whenever a man so acts, if we are to understand his action, we must know how he is better off (or thinks he is), or how the world is a better place (or is thought by him to be) as a result of what he does. He may explain this either by showing the badness of the preceding state of affairs or by showing the goodness of the (expected) succeeding state of affairs. Or again, he may classify his action as one of a well-known type productive of some specific form of amelioration.

Thus, the man who goes to the fire to get warm, if asked why he went to the fire, may say that he did so because he was cold, or that he did so in order to get warm. In the first case, the reason given is backward-looking; in the second case it has the form of the report of an intention. We might have, though in fact we have not, a brief general form of description for actions done to get warm because one is cold; we might call them "thermophilic actions". And the form which such a description of a particular action took might be this: we might say "He went to the fire *out of* thermophilia". And in such a case, we should say that we had given the *motive* of the man's action.

In this very simple case we can, I think, grasp the relationship between motive and intention. The important distinction is that between backward-looking

and forward-looking reasons for action. Reports of
intentions give forward-looking reasons for action;
reports of motives may *either* exhibit the action as
falling under some specific scheme of this general
pattern; *or* they may merely give a backward-looking
reason. Which backward-looking reasons we shall
naturally call "motives" depends on the comparatively trivial circumstance of whether or not we have a
name for the specific scheme exemplified.

One motive differs from another in accordance with
the different types of undesirability which can be
attributed to the pre-action state of affairs, and the
different types of desirability which can be attributed
to the post-action state of affairs. Thus, when A acts
out of fear of x the pattern which he exemplifies is
this: A is in danger of x—A acts—A is out of danger of
x. When A acts out of jealousy of B, the pattern is:
B is enjoying some benefit to the detriment of A—
A acts—B is not enjoying that benefit to the detriment
of A. In one sort of love, when A does something out
of love of B, then we have the pattern: B lacks some
good—A acts—B possesses the good which he lacked.
Each of these patterns is a particular specimen of the
general scheme: A is in a bad state—A acts—A is in
a good state. But the patterns of the particular
motives, though more specific than the general scheme,
are still of very wide generality; there are many
different kinds of danger, benefit, detriment, and so
forth. And the patterns should be complicated some-
what to allow for the possibilities of mistake at every
stage: the pattern for jealousy, for example, should
begin "B is (or is believed by A to be) enjoying some
benefit (or something believed by A to be a benefit)

to the detriment (or so A believes) of A ..." Again, the patterns sketched above leave much unexplained: why is it, for example, that B's lacking some good counts as A's being in a bad state? The pattern given for love is only a fragment of a larger pattern which would have to include some reference to A's wanting B to have whatever was good for him, and much else as well.

The general scheme, too, is inadequate as an account of intention: for A to act in order that p it is not sufficient that A should want that p and should believe that his action will bring it about that p. Some of the necessary complications will be considered in a later chapter; meanwhile, the scheme suffices for the purpose for which it was introduced, namely, to show the relation between intention and motive. By considering it we can see the reason for some of the puzzling features which we noticed earlier in the chapter. We can see why intentions can sometimes be deduced from motives and vice versa; for a report of an intention fills in in detail part of a pattern which a report of motive sketches out in general. We can see why "out of a desire to ..." does not assign a motive in the same way as "out of ambition", and why "because I wanted to ..." is not a backward-looking reason as "because he killed my father" is: for wanting is an element in *both* backward-looking and forward-looking reasons. We can see how it is that one can act from a motive without having the concept of it, and in what the sophistication of the concept of "motive" consists: acting in accordance with a particular pattern does not presuppose, and is presupposed by, naming the pattern in question. We can see why so many of

the names of motives are names of virtues and vices:
for the patterns of action which it most interests us to
single out and name are those by which we judge the
goodness or badness of an agent. We can see finally
why one can have a motive for an intention: for
forming an intention (in the sense of taking a decision)
is itself a human action which may fall into the
described pattern. On the other hand, the pattern itself
is not an action, and so one cannot have an intention
for a motive, though one can have a policy of acting,
or not acting, in accordance with a certain pattern,
and therefore an intention *to* act, or not act, out of
certain motives.

It depends on the way an action is described how
much there is left to be explained by reference to either
motive or intention. If we can see that a man is washing himself, we do not need to be told that he is
acting as he does because he wants to get clean, or
because he is dirty, or that he is acting out of cleanliness. The great majority of descriptions of human
actions carry with them built-in presumptions of this
kind about forward- and backward-looking reasons;
and one of the commonest functions of motive-words
is to cancel such presumptions. The kisses of Judas
need more explanation than the kisses of Romeo.

If a man is to explain his action by either forward- or
backward-looking reasons it is not always sufficient
for him merely to describe the wanted post-action
state of affairs or the unwanted pre-action state of
affairs. If the states of affairs are respectively obviously
good or obviously evil, this will suffice; otherwise, if
we are to understand his action we must be brought to
see the good or evil in question; it will not be enough

94

for him merely to say "I want this, and not that". Various levels of explanation and intelligibility are possible here. At one level of explanation an action, like any other event, is explained if it is shown as exemplifying some familiar pattern. So, in this sense, we understand a man's action once we see that he is acting in a way in which men often act, to bring about a state of affairs of a kind which men commonly like, or to put an end to a state of affairs of a kind which they commonly dislike. This, I think, is the truth behind Ryle's idea that an explanation in terms of motives stated a "law-like generalization". Being told that a man acted out of vanity helps us to understand his action not because (as Ryle thought) we say to ourselves "Yes, of course, he often acts like that", but because we say to ourselves "Yes, of course, *men* often act like that".

Now there are, I think, some cases where this is the *only* sort of understanding of an action possible. There are some unaccountable desires which many people have, such as the desire to throw themselves from high places or under approaching tube-trains. Such desires are no doubt not often acted on; but if told of a case, the only understanding one could have would be the thought "Yes, I have felt that too". Of course, one could seek for explanations of a physiological or psychoanalytic kind; but such explanation, if forthcoming, would not have the characteristics of an explanation of fully human action.

Hume thought that there were very many cases of this kind. "Besides good and evil, or, in other words, pain and pleasure, the direct passions frequently arise from a natural impulse or instinct, which is

95

perfectly unaccountable. Of this kind is the desire of punishment to our enemies, and of happiness to our friends; hunger, lust, and a few other bodily appetites" (*Treatise*, II, 3, 9).

In the case of hunger and 'lust', we can certainly reach fuller understanding than Hume thought; we can understand a man acting in order to assuage hunger not only because we know that men often act thus; we also know why they should act thus. Actions which are done to satisfy bodily needs, or to remedy bodily injuries, are as fully intelligible as any human actions can be. Actions motivated by sex do not in the same way serve any needs of the individual; but we understand them not only because we recognize the ubiquity of sexual desire, but also because we see its point.

So too with the commoner 'spiritual' desires; we know how honour, riches, and position serve human happiness, and so we understand actions done from vanity, cupidity, and ambition. But Hume's other cases—"the desire of punishment to our enemies, and of happiness to our friends"—raise interesting problems. There are two extremes to be avoided here; one must not pretend that serving one's friends or injuring one's enemies in no way serves one's own selfish purposes, nor must one pretend that the serving of these purposes is always one's intention in acting out of friendship or revenge. The motives here in question—the most difficult to explain on any account —are the most difficult to fit into the pattern we have given. What shall we say is the scheme when A kills B out of revenge? Is it: A looks like a man who can be injured with impunity—A acts—A does not look

like a man who can be injured with impunity? Or is it:
A has been injured by B and has not injured B—
A acts—A has been injured by B and A has injured
B? The first pattern attributes to A an intention
which he may not have at all, whereas the second
merely describes A's action twice without showing how
he is the better for it. As with revenge, so with friendship, obedience, admiration, and gratitude; actions
done out of these motives seem to produce no good for,
and remove no evil from, the agent. Here the usual
order is reversed; instead of an action done with a
certain intention exemplifying a pattern, we have an
action done *with the intention of exemplifying a pattern.*
It is significant that in these cases we can talk of an
action being done to *show* gratitude, or obedience, or
friendship; whereas an action done out of vanity is
not done to show vanity, and if an action is done to
display generosity it is not done out of generosity.
We can obtain further understanding of such actions
by considering the contribution which the pattern
exemplified by them—say, friendship and obedience—
can make or be thought to make to human well-being.
Whether a particular such pattern, e.g., revenge, is
the best, or a successful, or desirable, way of securing
the agent's happiness is another question.

Few, if any, actions bring about only the result
desired by the agent. An action which is done to bring
it about that *p* will bring it about also that *q* and that
r. The other results brought about may be states of
affairs which the agent does not want, or which are
bad for him, or which are injurious or displeasing to
others. Frequently there will be names of motives to
apply to these patterns also. A soldier who runs away

through fear may bring it about not only that he is no longer in danger but also that he is no longer in a position to carry out his orders; and so his action exemplifies the pattern not only of fear but also of cowardice. The child who eats five baskets of strawberries because it likes the taste exemplifies the pattern not of hunger but of gluttony. Similarly, no amount of information about a man's intentions will alone enable us to say whether he clung to a belief *out of pride* or not; whether pride came into it or not will depend partly on whether the belief was reasonable.

We may now bring together and amplify the conclusions of the last two chapters. Earlier, we agreed with Ryle in rejecting the idea that to act out of a certain motive was to act in consequence of the occurrence of the corresponding feeling. It would be nearer the truth to say that, on the contrary, a feeling is a feeling of a certain emotion only if it occurs in the context of an action fulfilling a certain motive-pattern. But this is not quite true, partly because feelings are linked more directly to the symptoms of an emotion than to motivated action. Trembling, blushing, psychogalvanic reflexes, and cardiac disturbances are symptoms of fear and shame; attempts to avert a danger or conceal a past crime are typical actions motivated by fear and shame. Actions, to be motivated, must be voluntary: symptoms, though sometimes checkable at will, are not normally producible at will. The symptoms of fear, or anger, or grief, where they occur do not greatly differ no matter what is feared, or gives rise to anger, or causes grief. Behaviour motivated by these emotions differs systematically in accordance with their object. The behaviour which is actuated by fear of getting fat is not the same as that which is actuated by fear of getting thin. Anger at a servant's slovenliness finds expression in action in a different manner from anger at a government's dishonesty. Feelings of emotion are the sensations linked with the symptoms of an emotion; but the sensations are feelings, just as the bodily changes are symptoms, only if they occur in a certain context. The context which attaches the sensations and the bodily changes to a particular emotion is itself specified as an emotional context by its relation to the pattern of action characteristic of the emotion in question. Going pale, for instance, is a symptom of fear only if it occurs in the face of at least putative danger; and danger is itself a backward-looking reason for actions which are motivated by fear. Thus feeling is linked to symptom, symptom to circumstance, and circumstance to action. The connection is roundabout, but every link in the chain is necessary.[1] The verbal expression of fear is linked to symptom, circumstance, and action; and once established, becomes itself a new criterion for the feeling.

[1] For instance, an animal who had a red light in his tail which glowed whenever he was in danger, could not be said to be showing symptoms of fear if he never made any attempts to avoid danger.

CHAPTER FIVE

DESIRE

ARISTOTLE, Aquinas, Descartes, and Hume all included desire among the passions of the soul. No doubt they were thinking of feelings of yearning or longing rather than of the often quite unemotional contexts in which we say 'I want . . .' Desire in the sense of wanting, unlike ἐπιθυμία and *desiderium*, is hardly an emotion: nevertheless, an account of it is essential to any treatment of the emotions. For the connection between emotions and behaviour is made by desire: one emotion differs from another because of the different sort of things it makes one want to do. Fear involves wanting to avoid or avert what is feared; anger is connected with the desire to punish or take vengeance on its object. Love, of one kind, is linked with the desire to fondle and caress the loved one, and shame with the desire to conceal whatever it is that makes one ashamed. These connections are not contingent: a man who was unaware of them would not possess the concept of the emotions in question.

Desire, in its most general sense, is not an emotion because it is not sufficiently closely connected with feelings. None the less, it has analogies with emotion, and we find the same philosophical positions main-

tained in its regard as we have seen exhibited in
connection with the emotions. On the one hand, desire
is sometimes thought of as a particular indefinable
sensation, whose unanalysable nature can be grasped
by each of us only by a mental gaze upon our own
experience. On the other hand, it may be regarded as a
recognizable pattern of behaviour, observed in the lives
of men and animals around us, and useful as a basis
for prediction of their future actions. We may call
these two extreme positions 'empiricist' and 'behaviourist' respectively. An empiricist will think that
wanting will be most helpfully clarified by comparison
with a visceral thrill or a lump in the throat; a
behaviourist will tend to illustrate the notion by
reference to animal performances of a fairly stereo-
typed nature, such as the courtship rituals of gulls.
In either case, the theorist may think of desire as a
phenomenon to which causal investigation of an
inductive nature may be applied without further
ado.

Few philosophers have adopted either of these
extreme positions without qualification. Russell, however, in the third chapter of his *Analysis of Mind*,
makes an interesting attempt to combine features of
both accounts. This may serve as a starting-point for
our discussion.

Russell begins by saying that the natural view on
this matter is to regard the content of a desire as being
just like the content of a belief. We will then think
that desire differs from belief simply in that the
attitude taken up towards the content is different.
"According to this theory when we say: "I hope it will
rain", or "I expect it will rain", we express, in the

101

first case, a desire, and in the second a belief, with an identical content, namely, the image of rain." It would be easy to say, he continues, that just as belief is one kind of feeling in relation to this content, so desire is another kind. Such a view, Russell feels, "cannot be refuted logically": it is only the phenomena revealed by psychoanalysis and the observation of animals which have led him to abandon it.

I think it is clear that this view which Russell treats with such respect is not so much 'the natural view' as 'the empiricist view'. The description of desire as 'a feeling' and the content of desire as 'an image' recall Hume's doctrine that desire was a direct passion, an impression, which arises from good "though conceived merely in idea" (*Treatise*, II, 3, 9). There will be occasion later to say something about the arguments which show that Hume's view is not as irrefutable as Russell believed. What is immediately interesting to notice is that Russell envisages no alternative to the Humean view other than the behaviourist view or a mixture of the two. He says that the discovery of unconscious desires by psychoanalysts shows us that desire must be "a causal law of our actions, not something actually existing in our minds". We can tell what animals want: hence "desire must be capable of being exhibited in actions, for it is only the action of animals that we can observe." For example, when we attribute thirst to an animal, on the basis of its behaviour, then our judgement is verified by the immediately succeeding action of the animal. "Most people would say that they infer first something about the animal's state of mind—whether it is hungry or thirsty and so on—and then derive their expectation

102

as to its subsequent conduct. But this detour through the animal's supposed mind is wholly unnecessary."

Russell therefore defines 'desire'—at least as far as concerns animals—in terms of 'behaviour cycles'. His definitions run:

A 'behaviour-cycle' is a series of voluntary or reflex movements of an animal, tending to cause a certain result, and continuing until that result is caused, unless they are interrupted by death, accident, or some new behaviour-cycle.

The 'purpose' of a behaviour-cycle is the result which brings it to an end, normally by a condition of temporary quiescence—provided there is no interruption.

An animal is said to 'desire' the purpose of a behaviour-cycle while the behaviour-cycle is in progress.

In giving an account of human desires, Russell introduces the further notion of 'discomfort'. Discomfort is a property of a sensation or other mental occurrence—a purely causal characteristic, consisting in the fact that the occurrence in question stimulates voluntary or reflex movements tending to bring about the cessation of the occurrence. In human beings, it is discomfort which starts off the behaviour-cycle in terms of which desire has been defined. Thus, in hunger, "we have first an uncomfortable feeling inside, producing a disinclination to sit still, a sensitiveness to savory smells, and an attraction towards any food that there may be in our neighbourhood". What is peculiar to conscious desire is that the discomfort and its subsequent behaviour-cycle are accompanied by a true belief as to the purpose of the cycle. It is this line of argument which leads Russell to his well-known conclusion that we can only really know what we want when we get it. He writes: "If our theory of desire is correct, a belief as to its purpose may very well be erroneous, since only experience can show what causes a discomfort to cease."

In this account Russell first rejects an empiricist account of desire on the grounds that we can ascribe desires not only to men but also to animals, and that even human desires may be unconscious. He then reintroduces empiricist elements when he comes to distinguish human desires from animal desires and conscious human desires from unconscious ones. We are left with a wholly behaviourist account of animal desire, a hybrid account of unconscious human desire, and a wholly, though covertly, empiricist account of conscious human desire.

Consider first what Russell says of unconscious human desires. Hunger, he remarks, may be such a desire: we may 'act with reference to food' before we say to ourselves "I am hungry"; the 'idea of food' need not be present during the entire behaviour-cycle of hunger. To say that a human being wants food is, for Russell, to assert a causal relationship between an internal impression ('a feeling inside') and a behaviour-pattern ('acting with reference to food'). It is essential to Russell's general position that 'a feeling inside' is not something which needs to be analysed behaviour-istically, but which carries its specification on its face. Hence Russell's account of unconscious human desires is reached by taking elements from two contrary philosophical theories and positing a causal relation between them. The result is that the 'behaviour-cycle' is not a behaviour-cycle at all; for what is to count

as its beginning is laid down not by reference to behaviour, but by reference to an internal impression.

In the account of conscious human wanting, though
the language of behaviourism is retained, the thought
becomes totally empiricist. Consider the sentence
quoted earlier: "Only experience can show what causes
a discomfort to cease." What does 'discomfort' mean
here? According to the definitions Russell has given
us, it should mean a causal characteristic of a mental
occurrence, namely, its stimulating certain behaviour.
If so, then to say that a discomfort ceases can only be
to say that the behaviour ceases. But if a man un-
consciously desires X, but falsely believes that he
desires Y, then the relevant behaviour-cycle will cease
not when he gets X, but when he gets Y. But in that
case, the distinction between true and false belief
will not achieve the distinction between conscious and
unconscious desires which it was introduced to effect;
for even in the case when the man is mistaken in
thinking that it is Y he wants, his discomfort (in this
sense) ceases when he gets Y. To be sure, the man won't
be *satisfied* when he gets Y, and will no doubt start a
new behaviour-cycle aimed at getting X, or even Z.
And this is clearly what Russell means: he means that
only experience can show what causes the *feeling* of
discomfort to cease. But he has no right to mean this
when he has defined discomfort not as a feeling but as
a causal characteristic.

But let us waive this, and allow Russell to say that
a man wants whatever it is which in fact brings his
feeling of discomfort to an end. Then, if a man believes
he wants X, and on getting X ceases to feel discomfort,
we must say that he genuinely wanted X; whereas, if he

believes he wants X, but does not cease to feel discomfort until he gets Y, we must say that *all along* he really wanted Y. But this means that it depends on what *feelings* a man has whether his original search for X and his subsequent search for Y are to count as two behaviour-cycles or as two parts of a single behaviour cycle. And now what is left of behaviourism when both the beginning and the end of a cycle of behaviour are determined by reference, not to behaviour, but to a private sensation? Desire is in effect being described in a purely Humean way by reference to a succession of two internal impressions.

So far, I have given no reason for thinking that either the behaviourist or the empiricist account of wanting is incorrect. At most I have given grounds for wondering why, if, like Russell, we give a behaviourist account of animal desire, and an empiricist account of conscious human wanting, we should call two so totally different things by the same name. I now wish to show that both the empiricist and the behaviourist accounts are mistaken, and to argue that the defects of each cannot be overcome by combining them with one another.

Consider first the behaviourist account, which Russell expounds in its most plausible context, that of animal desire. Desire in animals, he says, is displayed in a cycle of actions which are appropriate to a certain result and which are continued until the result is achieved. The difficulty about this definition is that such cycles of action are displayed also by inanimate beings and plants to which we do not attribute desire. The iron filings move towards the magnet, the rivers flow towards the sea, the tide ebbs and flows, the

apple-tree grows, buds, blossoms, and bears fruit.
Russell is aware of this difficulty, and of the analogous
one concerning the mechanical actions of animals
themselves. In the case of an animal falling over a cliff
to its death, he says, "we have, at first sight, just the
characteristic of a cycle of action embodying desire,
namely, restless movements until the ground is
reached, and then quiescence". It is to avoid these
difficulties that he defines a behaviour cycle as "a
series of voluntary or reflex movements *of an animal*"
which continue "*unless interrupted by death or accident*".
But by so qualifying his definition Russell merely calls
attention to the fact that we do not attribute desire
to inanimate objects, and that we distinguish between
accidents and results brought about on purpose. He
in no way explains why it is that the concept of desire
is inapplicable to inanimate objects, nor what is our
basis for distinguishing between accident and sought
result.

In fact, any piece of behaviour will have accidental
as well as desired consequences. In a sunny climate, for
instance, every movement of a bird from A to B will
cause a movement of the bird's shadow from A' to
B'. For all Russell's definition contains to the contrary, the change in place of the shadow might be the
purpose of the bird's movement, and its action in
flying to B might be described as "wanting its shadow
to be at B'."

Russell's definition is not only inadequate: it
contains a further qualification which makes it wholly
unusable. He allows that a behaviour-cycle may be
interrupted not only by death or accident, but also
by a new behaviour-cycle. The formal circularity of

107

his definition brings out the impossibility of explaining desire in terms of behaviour-patterns unless one can give an independent criterion for what is to count as a single behaviour-pattern. How is one to decide where one cycle ends and another begins? If an animal performs movements A, B, C, D in order, how is one to decide, without reference to the wants of the animal, whether this is one cycle designed to produce the consequences of D, or two cycles, one consisting of A and B and the other of C and D; or part of a cycle designed to produce the consequences of some further movement E which is interrupted after B by a further cycle, designed to produce the consequences of yet another movement F, which is itself interrupted after D? Appeal to 'quiescence' will not help us here. Each day of a dog's activity ends with sleep: but not every action of a dog's day exhibits a desire for sleep. On Russell's definition we should have to say this; unless we so tinker with 'tending to cause' as to smuggle purpose in by the back door. For there is certainly a causal connection between the dog's daytime activity and his sleep. He sleeps because he is tired; and he is tired because of whatever he did during the day.

Any purely behaviourist account of wanting is bound to fail. "Wanting" is not the name of a behaviour pattern as "flying" is, because what behaviour counts as the behaviour characteristic of wanting depends on what is wanted. Any behaviour whatsoever, regarded purely in itself, may be regarded as the manifestation of some want or other. There is nothing in a pure behaviourist theory to prevent us from regarding each piece of behaviour as a desire for whatever happens next. To prevent this, we need some criterion for deciding where one behaviour-pattern begins and another ends. Such a criterion is provided, in the case of animals, by their needs; and in the case of men, also by what they say. Something has already been said about needs; let us turn now to what Russell has to say about human wanting.

On Russell's view, if I am to say correctly that I want a cigarette, it must be the case:

(a) that I have a certain sensation—call it "S";
(b) that I exhibit cigarette-seeking behaviour (B);
(c) that S and B are causally connected;
(d) that I believe that smoking a cigarette will cause S to disappear;
(e) that my smoking does in fact cause S to disappear.

Now how is S to be identified? It cannot be identified as "the sensation of wanting to smoke a cigarette", for it will only be this if (e) is the case, and Russell is clearly prepared to allow that (a)–(d) might all be the case and (e) not. Is it identified as "the sensation which causes B"? No; for this would make the connection between S and B logical and not causal, which would falsify (c). Can it not be identified by a phenomenological description, say as "an unpleasant feeling in the throat"? No, for to say that it is unpleasant is, on Russell's view, simply to say that it is causally connected with B; which we have already ruled out.

There is one way out here which seems tempting: it is William James' way. Can we not say that S is the perception of B, or of part of B? Thus, we would have a way of identifying S by means of B which would yet allow them to be causally connected; provided, that is, that we are prepared to admit a causal theory of perception. Since Russell, in a later chapter of his book, substantially accepts James's theory of the emotions, it seems at first surprising that he does not mention it here. But the reason is obvious: on James' theory B, or part of B, is the cause of S; whereas Russell wants S to be the cause of B.

Let us suppose, however, that some method can be found of identifying S without reference to the other features of wanting; say by some purely neutral phenomenological description. How can the causal connection between S and B be established? Not by persons other than the subject of the experience; for they have no evidence for the occurrence of S other than the manifestation of B. The inductive correlation, if it is to be made, must be made by the person who has S.

In the case of many wants, it would be ludicrous to suggest that such a correlation could be made. Many people want water-colours to hang on their walls; but there is no single, independently identifiable sensation which is constantly conjoined with their water-colour seeking. But in the case of a cigarette, the suggestion is not obviously foolish; for there are sensations which are characteristic of the desire for a cigarette, such as a constriction of the throat and fidgetiness in the fingers. Could not a man inductively establish a connection between such feelings and subsequent cigarette-seeking behaviour?

Not on any simple 'constant conjunction' theory of causality. For it is possible to have the sensations without manifesting the behaviour: in Lent, or when one has become convinced of the danger of lung cancer. What then makes the difference between the cases where S is followed by B and those where it is not? If it is a decision of the agent, then the connec-

tion between S and B is not causal; if it is the presence
of some other causal factor Q then a description of
this factor is an essential element in any account of
wanting. But Russell gives no hint of what such a
factor might be.

Russell's account, as we have seen, is a sophistication of Hume's, according to which desire appears as a
particular sensation. The impossibility of treating
desire as a sensation is best brought out by asking
such questions as whether the same sensation occurs
when one wants a golliwog as when one wants some
chewing-gum. If so, then one wants to know why
chewing-gum will not satisfy the desire for a golliwog,
and vice versa; and in general, why any and every
object of desire will not satisfy any and every desire.
If on the other hand the sensations which occur in
connection with wanting a golliwog are quite unlike
those which are characteristic of wanting chewing-
gum, then it appears astonishing that we should use
the same word to refer to two such different sensations.
It is not as if "wanting" were a genus-word, like
"pain", to cover a broad class of varied sensations.
For any sensation whatever may be characterized as
appropriate to some want or other. To adapt a remark
of Wittgenstein's, if "wanting a golliwog" were the
name of a sensation, then it would not be a value of
the function "wanting X" and knowing the meaning of
"wanting a golliwog" would in no way help towards
the understanding of "wanting some chewing-gum"
(Cf. *The Blue Book*, 21).

We may now leave the empiricist and behaviourist
accounts of wanting, and prepare the way for a
positive account of our own.

The verb "want" may be followed by a direct object or by an infinitive: one may want an apple, a drink, a holiday, peace and freedom; one can also want to sneeze, to sing, to own a Bentley, to see Naples and to die. In many cases sentences of the form "I want X" (where X is an accusative following the verb "want") are expandible into sentences of the form "I want to ϕ X" (where X is an accusative following another verb "ϕ"). Thus, "I want an apple" often means "I want to eat an apple"; "I want a chair" means "I want to sit on a chair". Where the object of one's desire is something tangible, then the expression of one's wanting must be expandible in this way. A man may indeed want something without wanting it *for* anything, as collectors want curios; but no one can intelligibly say that he wants something if he cannot also say what counts as getting what he wants. The mere existence of a desired object is never enough to count as the gratification of a desire. Will the desire for an apple be satisfied by the apple's being placed within sight but not within reach? Will the desire for a chair be gratified by the loan of a chair, or only by the possession of a chair? Of course, in most cases there is no need to ask such questions; we know quite well that people normally want apples to eat and chairs to sit on. And, as my last sentence shows, the questions "what do you want it for?" and "what will count as getting it?" sometimes slide into one.

It is important to stress that the reason why we usually know offhand how to expand "he wants X" into "he wants to ϕ X" is because given the relevant substitution for "X" we know what to substitute for

112

"ϕ", not because there is some one common ϕ—say "to have in one's environment"—which can be attached to "wants" in all cases. That *to want* X is not *to want to have* X *in one's environment* is most clear in cases where what we substitute for "X" is not a word for a tangible object; as when we speak of a Wall Street financier wanting a revolution in Venezuela. But even in the case of tangible objects, the presence of a desired object in one's environment is neither a sufficient nor a necessary condition for the satisfaction of a desire. It is not a sufficient condition, for the presence of a bar of chocolate in the window of a closed shop will not gratify the desire for chocolate of a schoolboy flattening his nose against the pane outside. It is not a necessary condition, for a speculator who wants diamonds as a precaution against inflation may have his desire satisfied by their presence in a safe a thousand miles away.[1] If we want some general phrase to describe what counts as *getting* X where X is a tangible object desired we must say not "having X in one's environment" but "having X in one's power". But this is a possible description only because the word "power" is schematic in just the same way as the word "want". For "to have X in one's power" is simply "to be able to ϕ X"; and what "ϕ" is to be replaced by in any particular case depends on what the relevant X is.

If a man says that he wants a screwdriver, we know normally that he wants it to drive screws, and that his

---

[1] The possibility of such cases depends naturally on the existence of conventions governing property. For non-language-users it would be true to say that presence in the environment is a necessary, though not a sufficient, condition for satisfaction.

desire will be satisfied if and only if it is placed in such a position as to enable him to do this. This knowledge is based on our knowledge of what a screwdriver is, not on any information about the psychological processes of the wanter. To know the nature of a screwdriver, as of any artefact, is, among other things, to know what people normally want it for. Of course, someone may ask for a screwdriver because he wants to open a letter; but this is a case where we might say that he had imprecisely specified his want; anything with a sharp edge would do just as well. But might not a man want a screwdriver, and want it for driving screws, and yet make do with a paperknife? Yes: but this case differs from the case where he wants to open the letter. For if he wants to screw, if offered both a paperknife and a screwdriver, he will choose the screwdriver; if he wants to open a letter, he will choose the paperknife. So it seems that we can lay down some conditions for the specification of desires. Any utterance of the form "I want an X" completely specifies a want if and only if

(a) anything which is an X will satisfy the desire;
(b) nothing which is not an X will satisfy the desire better or equally well.

A man may want something without knowing what he wants it for; if, say, he has forgotten for the moment. *A fortiori* he may know that someone else wants something without knowing what that other person wants it for. It follows from what we have just said that such cases carry with them a vagueness about the object of the desire. A man who is shopping for his wife may well be nonplussed if told that X's are out of stock and asked whether Y's will do instead.

And if he is shopping from a list of his own and has forgotten why he wanted a piece of mahogany 5ft. × 3ft., he cannot begin to answer such questions as "will hardboard do?" But he could not do the shopping at all unless he knew that what counts in this context as "getting" is, e.g., having the purchases brought to the house.

We can, therefore, it seems, lay down some restrictions on possible objects of desire. Where X is a tangible object we may say:

(1) For "I want X" to be intelligible at all as the expression of a desire, the speaker must be able to answer the question "what counts as *getting* X?"

(2) For "I want X" to be a complete specification of a desire, the speaker must be able to answer the question "what do you want X for?"

These conditions lay down no absolute restriction on objects of desire; provided that they are both fulfilled, a name for any tangible thing may be substituted for "X".[1] There is at least one further condition which must be added; what is wanted must not be already in the wanter's power, or at least must not be known by him to be so. Aquinas pointed out that it is impossible to want what one already has as it is to

[1] Miss Anscombe seems to me to be wrong when she says that only present or future objects may be wanted (*Intention*, 69). Faustus' desire for Helen appears intelligible, genuine, and completely specified: he could answer the questions "what counts as getting Helen?" and "what will you do with Helen when you get her?" But perhaps Helen is not a 'past object' in Miss Anscombe's sense unless it is in some way logically impossible that she should be revived. In that case Faustus will be unable to specify what counts as "getting Helen" and his want will be ruled out by condition (1) above without our having to bring in, as Miss Anscombe does, a reference to time.

remember what is now happening (*Summa Theologica*, Ia IIae, 30, 2 ad 1). It follows that one can never want what one always has, e.g. one's own head. This obvious condition is sometimes strangely neglected by philosophers; as, for example, by Peter Abelard when in his hymn *O quanta qualia* he describes the joys of heaven:

> ubi non praevenit rem desiderium
> nec desiderio minus est praemium

Following Aquinas, we might say that a desire which did not precede its object would not be a desire, just as a memory contemporaneous with its object would not be a memory.[1]

What is wanted may be, not a tangible thing, but an experience: one may want a thrill, or an ecstasy, or the feeling of being taken out of oneself. But it would be misleading to say: in "A wants X" "X" may range over experiences as well as over tangible things. For where what is wanted is a sense-experience, then the natural form of expression does not allow of a direct object after a verb of wanting at all. We say not "He wants a visual experience of Vesuvius" but "He wants to see Vesuvius". The second expression is not only more natural, but also more accurate, since it provides no temptation to assimilate experiences to physical entities.

The only cases in which we have a natural form of expression in which a word for an experience occurs as

---

[1] Of course one can want *to keep* what one has; and this is often abbreviated simply to "want" in English; as in "do you want this old skirt?" said by somebody rummaging for things to give to a jumble sale.

the direct object of a verb of wanting are those in which a sensation-word contains in itself a desirability characteristic. Such expressions are "thrill", "ecstasy", "the pleasure of . . .", "the unusual experience of. . . ." The appearance that these words denote members of a special class of desirable sensations is illusory. To say that one went on the big dipper because one wanted a thrill is not to say that there was some special sensation, called a thrill, which one wanted over and above wanting to travel fast at dangerous angles, to see the ground rushing up at one, to feel one's stomach leaping, etc.; it is rather to justify one's desire for all these things by characterizing them as desirable in a certain way. Most such words, like "thrill" itself, have other uses besides desirability-characterizing ones. One can feel a thrill of horror as well as a thrill of joy; though this does not mean that one could feel a thrill and then wonder whether it was a thrill of joy or a thrill of horror.

There is no ground, then, for admitting sensations as a special class of *desiderabilia* along with tangible things. For any sentence which contains the name of a sensation as an accusative after a verb of desire expresses either, or both,

(a) a desire to do or undergo certain things;

(b) a justification for a desire of type (a).

In cases where we have a sentence of the form "I want X" and "X" is the word for a sensation, if it cannot be treated as an expression of either (a) or (b) then it is quite unintelligible. As would be "I want a gentle throbbing sensation in my left calf" if the speaker could give no instructions how the sensation was to be caused and no account of what was the fun of it.

DESIRE

But what of the masochist? Is he not defined as a man who desires pain; and is not pain a sensation? Yes; but the masochist's desire for pain must be capable of expression as a desire to suffer quite specific treatment at the hands of a specific type of person. Otherwise it becomes not merely odd, but unintelligible. Pain is identified as such partly by its cause and partly by the subject's reaction to it. Since the masochist's reaction to his sensation is not a pain-reaction, the only reason that we have for calling it "pain" is that it is caused by treatment which from other men elicits pain-reactions. If, therefore, the masochist cannot specify how what he wants is to be produced, there is no reason to call the object of his desire "pain". His "I want pain" will then tell us nothing. The other possibility of understanding expressions of desire for sensations—namely, as desirability-characterizations of certain activities, or undergoings—is here ruled out, since to call something painful is to characterize it as *un*desirable.

Besides sensations and tangible things one can want many other things: haircuts, fine weather, health, revolutions, laws and repeals of laws, more free time, less petty restrictions, room to live in, brighter colours and gayer fashions, and so on until we exhaust Aristotle's categories and Roget's thesaurus. But all such desires are expressible as desires to do or undergo certain things, or for certain states of affairs to come to pass. For the fundamental use of "want" we are left with two candidates: "wanting to ϕ" and "wanting X to ϕ".

These we must now consider. We have already seen that desires for tangible things and for sensations

118

must be analysable into expressions of the form "I want to ϕ (X)". Are there restrictions on what one can want to do analogous to those which we laid down for wanting tangible things? The first was that in order to say "I want X" intelligibly, a speaker must be able to say what counted as *getting* X. *A pari,* if he is to say "I want to ϕ" intelligibly, then he must be able to say what counts as ϕ-ing. But this is merely to say he must understand the words he uses; which is a condition of intelligibility for any utterance at all. Therefore, in the case of "I want to ϕ" our first condition lapses.

The second condition was that for "I want X" to be complete specification of a desire, the speaker must be able to say what he wants X *for.* The parallel condition here would be that in order for "I want to ϕ" to be the complete specification of a desire, the speaker would have to be able to say why he wanted to ϕ. Where ϕing is a means to an end, this condition holds: but ϕing may be desired for its own sake. If that is so, then types of answer are appropriate to "why do you want to ϕ" which were insufficient to answer "what do you want an X for?" "Because ϕing is pleasant" is a complete answer to the first question in a way in which "because X's are pleasant" is not to the second. For the second answer must be completed by saying that X's are pleasant to taste, or to look at, or to carry in the hand, or whatever.

The first two restrictions on wanting therefore lapse with regard to "wanting to ϕ".

The third restriction, however, has an analogue here. Just as one cannot want what one has already got, or what one always has, so one cannot want to do what one is already doing, or always does. I cannot want to yawn while I am yawning, or want to smoke while I am smoking, or want to be an engine-driver when I am already an engine-driver. Nor can I want to be a human being, or to circulate my blood, or to live in the twentieth century, or to weigh more than air. In the first set of cases, the question "do you want to ϕ?" gives place to such questions as "do you like ϕ-ing?" "are you enjoying ϕ-ing?" "do you want to go on ϕ-ing?" "do you want to ϕ again?" In the second set of cases, talk of enjoyment seems as out of place as talk of desire.[1]

It is, of course, possible to want to do what one is already doing, if one does not know that one is doing it. One can want to meet Professor X when Professor X is in fact the bore from whom one is trying at this moment to escape. Nebuchadnezzar, under the delusion that he was a beast, no doubt wanted intensely to be a human being. Again, one can be finding one's braces and want to find them; be winning a game and at the same time wanting to win it. But that is because one may be finding one's braces and yet not find them; be winning a game and lose it after all. With these qualifications, it is true that I can want to ϕ only if I am not ϕ-ing. Are there any other restrictions on what one can want to do? Can one, for instance, want to do what one cannot do?

There is clearly some connection between the ability to ϕ and the ability to want to ϕ. Beings which cannot

[1] One can, of course, want to *go on* doing what one is doing; and one can do what one *wanted* to do. There is also a sense in which one can *be doing* what one wants to do; but this sense, which will be considered later, is not directly connected with desire.

drink cannot be thirsty, and beings who cannot speak cannot feel an urge to swear. Only a man who can play chess can want to castle, and a newborn baby cannot want to pray. On the other hand, we cannot say that a man can want to ϕ only if he can ϕ. We have to want to swim before we learn to swim, and one does not need wit to want to make others laugh. The foodless victims of a siege feel hunger, and the blind man in the Gospel wanted to see.

It is clear that different types of ability and possibility are here in question. A full discussion of these would take us too far round: the following points seem relevant to our present topic.

Can a man want what is logically impossible? It seems not, for the following reason. Wanting finds expression in two ways: verbally, and in behaviour. The verbal expression of wanting involves a description of the state of affairs wanted; but what is logically impossible is indescribable. The behavioural expression of wanting consists in steps taken towards a desired end; but there are no steps towards a logically impossible end.

Since one can be mistaken about what is logically impossible, it follows that there is a sense in which one can be mistaken about what one wants. Some may find this an unpalatable conclusion, and try to avoid it in the following way. There are indeed no steps towards a logically impossible end; but may there not be behaviour which is mistakenly believed to be such a step? Suppose a man says that he wants to travel backwards in time, and builds a vehicle for this purpose, packs chain-mail in his trunk and steps aboard: have we not here enough grounds for saying

I

that he wants what is logically impossible? No: for whenever we try to specify the object of his want, we are condemned to utter nonsense or to contradict ourselves. As for the possibility of being mistaken about what one wants, this can exist in other cases too: for the description of the object of a want may be a misdescription just as it may be a merely putative description.

In denying the possibility of wanting what is logically impossible, I am not denying the possibility of having incompatible wants. Because it is impossible for a man to want that both p and not-p, it does not follow that it is impossible for him both to want that p and to want that not-p. For we cannot in general say that if A wants that p and A wants that q, then A wants that p and q. Again we cannot say that if A wants that p and if "p" implies "q", then A wants that q, any more than we can say that if A believes that p and if "p" implies "q", then A believes that q. In practice, whether a man can harbour incompatible desires, or subscribe to incompatible beliefs, depends on how obviously incompatible they are. And of course however incompatible two desires may be, one may always wish that they were *not* incompatible.

Animals, lacking language, can express wants only by behaviour. It follows that they can want to do only what they can in general do and sometimes do; for there could be no reason to regard behaviour which was never followed by ϕing as a manifestation of the desire to ϕ. This is not to say that no individual animal could ever display a want to do what he has enver done and perhaps cannot do; but he can want to do only those things which animals of his kind can do and do.

Language-users, on the other hand, can want not only what they can try to do, but also what they can describe. What a man can neither describe nor try to do he cannot want to do: that is why the man who cannot play chess cannot want to castle. Various combinations are possible here: one may want to do what one can describe but cannot try to do (the blind man wanting to see), or one may want to do what one can try to do but cannot describe (e.g. to produce a quite particular expression in playing a musical passage). In the standard case, what is wanted can be both described and attempted; in such a case the genuineness of the verbal expression of desire is measured by the vigour of the attempts to fulfil it. Besides being describable and attemptable, a desired activity must normally be characterizable as desirable by reference to recognized human goods.[1]

Such, then, are the conditions of intelligibility for expressions of desire of the form "I want to φ", and reports of desires of the form "A wants to φ". There are also desires which are reported in the form "A wants X to φ", as in "John wants the weather to be fine", "James wanted Peter to marry Mary". The natural verbal expression of these wants need not contain any reference to the speaker at all: he may say simply "If only the weather keeps fine!" or "Peter should marry Mary". And the reports may take a form akin to *oratio obliqua*: "John is anxious that the

[1] There are some things, but not many, which one can 'just want' to do, for no particular reason. Cf. Miss Anscombe, *Intention*, 26, 69 ff.

weather should keep fine", "James desired that Peter should marry Mary".

Desires of the "wanting to ϕ" form may be regarded as a particular case of this form: as wanting oneself to ϕ, wanting that one should ϕ. There will be some cases where this will be quite a natural form of expression, as in "He wants himself to be elected Chairman"; others in which it would be very odd, as "he wants that he should sneeze".

There is, in fact, an important distinction between the senses of "want" involved in these two cases. There are wants where what is wanted is wanted for *now*, and the desire is unsatisfied, and perhaps grows, until what is wanted is obtained. Such wants are hunger, thirst, sleepiness, and sexual desire. Other wants look forward to a perhaps remote date; as one can now want to go to Greece next summer, or to marry a girl once one has found a job. Such wants are not frustrated every moment until the awaited day arrives; they are in one sense satisfied as soon as one has certainty that they will be realized. All animal wants are of the first, immediate variety; long-term wants are peculiar to language-users (Cf. Aquinas, *Summa Theologica*, I, 95, 2c).

The form of description "wanting to ϕ" is fully adequate to describe a want of the first kind, where the time of what is wanted is the same as the time of the wanting. It is not similarly adequate to describe a want of the second kind. "I wanted to go to London yesterday" is ambiguous between:

(1) [At some unspecified time] I wanted to go yester-
    day to London

and

(2) Yesterday I wanted to go [at some unspecified time] to London.

The direct-object form of description is even more inadequate: the ambiguity of "I wanted a holiday yesterday" can be brought out only by rewriting it as "I wanted to take a holiday yesterday" and making explicit the time-references as in (1) and (2) above.

Since time and tense of wanting can differ from time and tense of what is wanted, the only fully clear method of reporting those wants which are peculiar to language-users is by the use of a clause to describe the object of the want. Such forms will not usually be natural, since we commonly rely on context to clear up ambiguities such as that between (1) and (2); and the use of tensed infinitives and manipulations of word-order can serve the purposes served by the tense and other qualifications of the verb in a *that* clause. In reports of wishes, however, the *that*-clause is a quite natural way of bringing out differences between the time and tense of the wish and the time and tense of its object: "When he grows up, he will wish that he had gone to a better school."

Similar complications arise over negation. If I say "I don't want cod" I may mean either that I would not go out of my way to get cod, or that I would go out of my way to avoid cod; the difference in spoken English is brought out by emphasis. It can be made clear by the use of *that*-clauses.

(3) I do not want that I should eat cod.

(4) I want that I should not eat cod.

There are two other possible attitudes I may have about cod:

(5) I want that I should eat cod.

(6) I do not want that I should not eat cod.

(3) and (5) are contradictories and so are (4) and (6). But (4), though it excludes (5), is not the contradictory of it; both (4) and (5), may be false together, if I don't care either way about cod. The logical relations between these sentences exhibit a familiar pattern: they can be exhibited in a 'square of opposition' like that for quantified, modal, and deontic propositions.[1] Writing "W" for "I want that" and "*p*" for "I shall eat cod" we have:

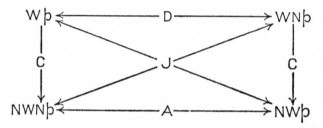

Reports of the desires of language-users, therefore, though they sometimes look as if they expressed a relation between a wanting subject and a desired thing, in fact fall into the class of sentences which Russell has called "propositions with more than one verb".[2] Before propounding a theory of desire to conform to the conditions laid down in this chapter, we must wait until we have approached two-verb sentences from a different angle.

[1] Cf. Prior, *Formal Logic*, 220. This scheme ignores the possibility just mentioned of inconsistent desires. It exhibits the pattern which *would be* exemplified if everyone was self-consistent.

[2] *Logic and Knowledge*, 216 ff. The most notorious sub-class of this class is the class of reports of beliefs.

CHAPTER SIX

PLEASURE

A CONSIDERATION of desire leads naturally to the topic of pleasure. The two concepts are connected in ways which are reflected by the truisms that men want to do what they enjoy doing and enjoy doing what they want to do. If a man likes ϕing, this comes out when he is not ϕing in his wanting to ϕ, and when he is ϕing in his enjoying ϕing. Beings which cannot want to do anything cannot enjoy doing anything; shrubs, stocks, and stones, bereft of pleasure, are free also from desire.

But the concept of pleasure is more complicated than that of desire. Wanting to ϕ is obviously not the same as ϕing; between enjoying ϕing and ϕing the distinction is not so clear. Enjoyment may be thought of as distinct from, or as identical with, what is enjoyed. Some philosophers, like Bentham, have taken the former view; others, like Ryle, have taken the latter; Aristotle perhaps attempted to take both together. Each view finds support in our natural way of speaking: eating and drinking are pleasures, and also give pleasure; "He took pleasure in nothing but Ludo" will do as well as "Ludo was his only pleasure".

We get pleasure out of pleasures, and derive enjoyment from enjoyments.[1]

Those who regard pleasure as a concomitant of action usually think of it as a sensation. Freud, for example, talks of "mental processes being accompanied by pleasure" and states that "what consciousness yields consists essentially of excitations coming from the external world and of feelings of pleasure and unpleasure which can only rise from within the mental apparatus."[2]

Undoubtedly there are some pleasures which are sensations. Sexual pleasure is localized in the body as hunger and thirst are; one may feel pleasure from a caress as one may feel pain from a blow. There are glows of pleasure as there are stabs of pain; the felt warmth of the fire may change insensibly from a delight to a discomfort.[3]

But though some sensations are pleasant, pleasure is not in general a sensation. To say that some event was enjoyed is not to say that it was accompanied by a specific sensation named "pleasure"; for no sensation is specified merely by being called pleasant. Moreover, if pleasure were a sensation its connection

[1] There are other concepts where we oscillate between identification-language and concomitant-language. Our interests awake our interest, disappointments give rise to disappointment, and griefs cause us grief.

[2] *Beyond the Pleasure Principle*, 24 (Vol. 18. of the Collected Works).

[3] Since pleasure may be a sensation, and pain need not be, pain and pleasure are perhaps not as ill-assorted a pair as they are sometimes said to be, e.g., by Ryle. Before Ryle, Albertus Magnus argued that pain and pleasure were not contraries, on the ground that those who scratch themselves when they itch feel pain and pleasure with the same sense in the same place at the same time (*Summa de Bono*, III, V. 3).

with what produced it would be a causal one. It would thus be only as a result of induction that we could say on any given occasion what we were enjoying. It would be possible to make exactly the same mistakes about what was giving one pleasure as it is possible to make about what has given one a stomach-ache. If, say, one had enjoyed listening to the first performance of a new overture, it would be a mere hypothesis that what one had enjoyed was listening to the overture and not, say, sitting in row G of the dress circle. This hypothesis would need to be verified in accordance with Mill's canons: one should listen to the overture again, sitting in row F of the stalls, and introspect carefully to see if the same sensation occurred.[1]

This is clearly absurd, but it may be objected that it is a tendentious example. Surely, it may be said, there are cases where we do make mistakes about the object of our enjoyment, and cases where we have to repeat an experience in order to find out what it is about it that causes us pleasure. Thus a man might say that he enjoyed the scenery on his honeymoon, when it was really the company of his bride which he had enjoyed; and he might realize this through visiting the locality alone at a later date. The music-lover replays the record to discover whether what made that passage so delightful was the exotic syncopation or the unconventional modulation. In the face of such every-day cases—to say nothing of the more elaborate types of self-deception unmasked by psychoanalysts and confessors—how can we deny that it is sometimes by

[1] The argument in this and the following paragraphs is a development of one used by Ryle in *Dilemmas*.

induction that we discover what we really enjoyed on a given occasion?

The cases given are not, in fact, an objection to our thesis. Any human action is capable of more than one description; it may be described in greater or less detail, and it is difficult to set *a priori* boundaries between the details which count as part of the description of an action and the details which count merely as descriptions of its circumstances. Now an action may be enjoyed under one description and not under another. Various cases are possible here: the most obvious is where a man does not know that his action falls under a certain description because of some ignorance of fact. Thus, Oedipus enjoyed making love to Jocasta, but he did not enjoy making love to his mother, because he did not know that Jocasta was his mother. There is no difficulty here, because although he was mistaken about what he did, he was not mistaken about what he enjoyed. For a man can only enjoy doing what he knows he is doing; which does not mean that he can only enjoy what he knows he is enjoying.

A different case is that in which the agent is in no ignorance concerning the facts, but would reject a certain description of his action through self-deception. Thus an employee might enjoy telling her employer that one of her fellow-employees had robbed the till; and she might describe this as "deriving satisfaction from doing her duty". She would reject the accusation that she was enjoying retailing gossip, because she would reject this as a description of what she was doing.

There is a third case. A schoolboy at a dormitory

feast imagines that he is enjoying eating cold bacon and burnt potatoes when he is really enjoying the illicitness of his escapade. This case differs from the previous one, for the schoolboy would not reject "breaking rules" as a description of what he was *doing*, but merely as a description of what he was *enjoying*.[1]

Both the tale-bearing employee and the rule-breaking schoolboy might later come to revise their account of what it was they enjoyed. And they might be led to make such a revision by some process very like that of inductive refutation of a hypothesis. The employee may find that she derives no satisfaction from reporting defaulters whom she does not dislike; the schoolboy discovers that chill greasy food loses all its attractiveness if served in the refectory.

But in both cases the mistake and the revision concern not the identity of the action enjoyed, but the appropriate description of the activity, *qua tale* or *qua* enjoyed. In all such cases there is a sense in which the action originally misreported, and the action later correctly described, are one and the same action. In no case where two completely independent actions are being performed simultaneously is the agent ever in doubt which of them he is enjoying. But such doubt would be possible if pleasure were a sensation concomitant on and merely contingently connected with action.

Earlier, in arguing that desire was not a sensation, I suggested that it was impossible to regard desire either as a single sensation or as a sensation which differed every time the object of desire differed. A

[1] Cf. Gosling. "False Pleasures in the *Philebus*" (*Phronesis*, 4, 44–54).

similar argument may be put forward against the thesis that pleasure is a sensation. If pleasure is a sensation, then either it is always and everywhere the same sensation, or else it is a genus comprising perhaps as many different specific sensations as there are different objects of pleasure.

Aristotle suggested the following argument to show that pleasure is not a single uniform sensation. Actions are performed better if accompanied by pleasure than if not. The more we enjoy doing philosophy, then, other things being equal, the better we philosophize. But if pleasure is always and everywhere the same, then an action will be improved if accompanied by pleasure derived from whatever source. Therefore we shall philosophize better if while philosophizing we are thoroughly enjoying our favourite concerto. But in fact, activities are hindered by pleasures derived from other activities: as Aristotle pointed out, flute-lovers cannot follow an argument if the flute is being played next door. Music while you work is a poor substitute for enjoying your job (*Nicomachean Ethics*, X, 1175 a 21–b 7).

But why should not pleasure be a genus comprising many specific sensations? Protarchus, in Plato's *Philebus*, says that if pleasures derived from different sources are themselves unlike in kind, it is strange that they are all called by the same name. To this Socrates retorts that one might as well argue that black is the same as white, since they are both called colours.[1]

---

[1] *Philebus*, 12 b 6 ff. Professor Hackforth's commentary on this passage is an interesting example of the effect of reading Plato with Humean eyes. Plato, he suggests, allowed Socrates to argue fallaciously by using "pleasure" ambiguously, so that it sometimes means "pleasant feeling *per se*" and sometimes "the complex of

But the relation of colour to colours is not the same as the relation between pleasure and pleasures. One learns what colour is by learning to distinguish black from white and other colours; one does not learn what pleasure is by learning to discriminate between the pleasures of golf and the pleasures of sonneteering. Still, one does not acquire a concept of pain by learning to tell a headache from a toothache; for all that, physical pain is a genus of sensations of which headaches and toothaches are species. And if pain, why not pleasure?

There can be no objection to saying that pleasure is a genus of sensations if all that is meant is that some sensations may be classified as pleasant, and that some among the various specific pleasures are sensations. The view here being attacked is the view that what makes *any* event or action pleasant is its being accompanied by one or another of a set of specific sensations, in the way in which the writing of an essay may be made painful by its being accompanied with a headache. On such a view, the connection between the particular sensations and the objects which produce them would have to be learnt by experience. It would be quite a contingent matter that the pleasure of drinking did not occur while one was eating, nor the pleasure of climbing the Matterhorn while one was toasting crumpets.

This theory, like others of its kind, breaks down

pleasure and source of feeling". This was because Plato thought that the feeling aroused by hearing great music was qualitatively different from that aroused by eating sweets, but could not prove this. At bottom, Hackforth says, the question is one for experimental psychology to pronounce upon (*Plato's Examination of Pleasure*, 15–16).

through the impossibility of providing any suitable criterion for the occurrence of the sensations which it posits. If the sensations are supposed to stand in need of no criterion of identification, then they are internal impressions, and are exposed to all the general arguments against internal impressions. In particular, an internal impression could never be a reason for action, whereas pleasure is always a reason for action.[1] Pleasure, in the nature of things, is desirable; but no internal impression could be shown *a priori* to be desirable. For if "this is desirable" means "this ought to be desired" then it cannot be inferred from a descriptive premise "this is an impression of such-and-such a kind", under pain of that naturalistic fallacy which believers in internal impressions so vehemently decry.[2] On the other hand, if "desirable" means "*de facto* desired by all or most men" then the assertion that the impression of pleasure is desirable must wait upon statistical research. And in each individual case "because I enjoy it" is no longer a terminating answer to the question "why do you do that?" because we can always go on to ask whether our interlocutor is one of those men who find this reported impression desirable. And if he answers in the affirmative, then this answer too is incomplete; for on an empiricist view desire no less than pleasure is an internal im-

---

[1] I do not mean that a thing's being pleasant is always a *sufficient* reason for doing it; there may be strong reasons for abstaining. I mean merely that it is always silly to ask a man why he wants pleasure.

[2] Refutations of Utilitarianism, which accuse it of committing the naturalistic fallacy by treating "good" as being the same sort of predicate as "yellow", frequently commit the same fallacy by treating "pleasant" as if it was the same sort of predicate as "yellow".

pression. We are merely multiplying impressions without ever finding a ground for action.

If "pleasure" is not the name of a sensation, it is not the name of a behaviour-pattern either. To say that an activity is pleasant if and only if it is accompanied by a smile is just as foolish, and more obviously so, as to say that an activity is pleasant if and only if accompanied by a particular sensation. To be sure, pleasure has an influence on behaviour; but there is no behaviour, characteristic of enjoying something, which can be identified separately from the behaviour characteristic of what is enjoyed. What behaviour counts as characteristic of *enjoying φing* depends on what φing is; just as what behaviour counts as *trying to φ* depends on what φing is.

One test of whether a man is enjoying something is to see whether he goes on doing what he is doing, or whether he tries to do it again. But if we could define enjoyment as a tendency to prolong or repeat, we should still not have succeeded in giving a behaviourist account of it; for prolonging and repeating are not patterns of behaviour any more than trying, beginning, and imitating are. In any case, the definition will not do; there are so many cases where the prolongation or repetition of what was enjoyed would ruin the enjoyment. The sweetest last to make the end most sweet might not be sweet were it not also last. Enjoying a play does not mean wishing that it had six acts instead of five, and one can enjoy the first movement of a symphony without being distressed that it is followed by the second.

"When one does something with enjoyment" it is sometimes asked, "what does one do which one doesn't

do if one just does it without enjoyment?" The
question is too schematic to be answered as it stands.
Once it is made specific, it seems easily and trivially
answerable. For example: "What is the difference
between eating a chop and enjoying it, and just eating
a chop?" We may reply: in the one case one toys with
one's food, pulls faces, sighs, leaves a good deal on
one's plate; in the other case one eats with animation,
is distracted from the conversation, scrapes the last
bit of meat from the bone and sighs contentedly at the
finish. "Yes, but now one is *not* doing the same thing
in the two cases, once we describe fully what is done.
What we wanted was a case where two activities were
exactly the same, save only that one was enjoyed and
the other was not."

One possible reaction to this is to deny that there
could be such a case. Hare has remarked that one
cannot say of two paintings P and Q "P is exactly like
Q in all respects save this one, that P is a good picture
and Q not" (*The Language of Morals*, 80–81). Can we
not equally object to saying "Today's game of golf
was exactly like yesterday's, except that I enjoyed
yesterday's and I did not enjoy today's"? Aquinas
was prepared to maintain that if you do a thing once
and enjoy it, and do it again and fail to enjoy it, then
you cannot really have done the same thing twice.
When people first look at a landscape, he said, they
enjoy it because they scrutinize it; but when they are
used to it, they do not look so carefully, and therefore
they feel less pleasure.[1]

It is certainly true that in general we are expected
to give some reason for not enjoying something which

[1] See Aquinas' commentary on Aristotle's *Ethics*, 1175 a 5–10.

we usually enjoy doing. On the other hand, it is certain that of two actions both of which conform to a single description, one may be enjoyed and the other not. Even if it is true that in such cases there is always some more detailed description which fits only one of the actions in question, a man may often say whether he enjoyed what he did without being able to give a fuller description. And even when he can give such a description, giving the fuller description is far from being another way of saying that the action under the vaguer description was enjoyed. For, once again, to say that one enjoys doing something is to give a reason for doing it; but one does not give a reason for doing something merely by describing more precisely what one is doing. Pleasure, then, is not some extra activity over and above the activity *in* which it is pleasure.

Seeing the impossibility of defining pleasure as a sensation or activity accompanying the action enjoyed, some philosophers have been tempted to regard it as identical with the action. Thus Ryle:

To say that a person has been enjoying digging is not to say that he has been both digging and doing or experiencing something else as a concomitant or effect of the digging; it is to say that he dug with his whole heart in his task; i.e. that he dug, wanting to dig and not wanting to do anything else (or nothing) instead. His digging was a propensity fulfilment. His digging was his pleasure, and not a vehicle of his pleasure (*The Concept of Mind*, 108).

Certainly, having failed to reach any satisfactory answer to the question, "When something is enjoyed, what happens which does not happen when it is not

K

137

enjoyed?" we are tempted to think that the right question may be "When something is enjoyed, what *does not* happen which *does* happen when it is not enjoyed?" To this question many answers suggest themselves. If I am enjoying something I am not feeling bored, or thinking of other things, or wishing it was over, or suffering from a headache, or feeling tired. With these answers we do not get into the difficulties which beset us when we were trying to answer the earlier question. For being bored is very much the same no matter what one is bored with, in a way in which enjoyment is not the same no matter what is enjoyed. And a stomach-ache spoils one's pleasure in a performance of *Hamlet* no less than in a Christmas pudding. Being bored with life is related to being bored with a conversation as disposition to episode; whereas enjoying exhibitions and enjoying a particular exhibition are not so related. A voluntary activity, we might say on this view, is enjoyed unless there is some specific reason to the contrary. An activity is innocent of unpleasure until it is proved guilty. Thus we arrive at a definition of pleasure similar to that given by Aristotle in the seventh book of the *Ethics*: pleasure is unimpeded operation.[1]

Such an approach illuminates many things, but not everything. It still leaves unanswered the question: why is pleasure a reason for action? Again, there are many unimpeded actions which are not enjoyed, and not all the things which we enjoy are, by Aristotle's account, "operations". There are many things which we do which we neither enjoy nor dislike; most

[1] 1153 a 15. I use "operation" purely as a synonym for "ἐνέργεια." See Chapter 8 below.

obviously, actions performed more or less from habit such as shaving or walking to work. Asked whether one had enjoyed such things, one would not answer yes, and one would not answer no; one would merely give a shrug. Saying that shaving is neither enjoyed nor disliked is not like saying that virtue is neither fast nor slow. We are not drawing attention to any category mistake. For an action which is commonly neutral in this way may, in suitable circumstances, give rise to enjoyment or dislike. Normally one does not enjoy or dislike walking to work; given an exceptionally fine morning or a violent thunderstorm one may feel quite strongly about it. In the case of such actions, one would be expected to give a reason either for saying that one had enjoyed them or for saying that one had not enjoyed them. The mere absence of reasons for saying that one has enjoyed them is not a sufficient reason for saying that one has not enjoyed them, and vice versa.

There are, however, *some* actions of which the account in *Ethics* VII holds; there are some actions which are enjoyed in the absence of any special reason to the contrary. It is these actions which most deserve to be called pleasures. An enquiry into pleasure cannot therefore be complete without giving some account of what makes an action a member of this class.

Before attempting this, we must meet an objection which calls in question our whole procedure so far. "What is pleasure?" is an intractable question, it may be suggested, because it is not sufficiently linguistic. Replace it with the question "How is the word "enjoy" used?" and the difficulties will disappear. Modern techniques of distinguishing between descriptive and evaluative language will solve the problems, and dissolve the puzzles, which baffled earlier philosophers who wrote on pleasure.

Typical of this attitude is Professor Nowell-Smith's treatment of pleasure in his *Ethics*. Briefly, his theory is that where "pleasure" is used so that pleasure seems not to be identical with action, it is being used evaluatively; where pleasure appears to be identical with action, then "pleasure" is being used descriptively.

The word "pleasure" can certainly be used to refer to certain activities, such as dancing, drinking and dicing, without betraying any liking for them. When Puritans denounce pleasure, they are commonly denouncing specific pastimes, and we would not say that a hermit was living a life of pleasure even if he thoroughly enjoyed fasting. When "enjoy yourself" is a piece of advice and not a wish it is an example of a similar use of "enjoy". No doubt such activities are called pleasures partly because most men enjoy them most of the time. But one can call them "pleasures" purely descriptively in the sense that by so referring to them one need not be giving any clue to one's own likes and dislikes.

Nowell-Smith, however, seems in error in thinking that the distinction between descriptive and evaluative uses will solve the problems about pleasure. He writes:

"Enjoyment" is neither the name of a type of disposition nor the name of a type of occurrence. It is primarily a pro-word the function of which is to block the question "Why did you do that?" (*Op. cit.*, 132).

This seems oversimplified. There are many other uses of "enjoy"; in particular, the many uses of "I did not enjoy . . ." which are hardly intended to *un*-block the question "Why did you do that?" But more importantly, it does not seem that the part which pleasure plays in our lives can be most helpfully elucidated by pointing to the part which an utterance such as "I enjoy it" plays. In general, the circumstances in which a man ϕs do not coincide with the circumstances in which it will be natural for him to *say* "I am ϕing." If you have an ugly face, then this fact alone will justify me in thinking that you have an ugly face; it will not justify me in *saying* "I think you have an ugly face." This complication is of particular importance in a consideration of pleasure. One of the significant features of pleasure is that people will do things for the sake of it; but this feature cannot be set in its true light merely by considering the circumstances in which people will *say* that they are doing something for the sake of pleasure.

If other accounts of pleasure fail because they ignore the fact that pleasure can be a reason for action, Nowell-Smith's account fails because he is too preoccupied with this fact, and because he confuses *being motivated by pleasure* with *giving pleasure as one's motive*. The use of "enjoy" which he singles out as primary is one of its least typical uses. "Because it is pleasant" is not often given as a serious reply to the question "Why do you do that?" It rather suggests that the question was a silly one to ask. Indeed, if it is silly to ask someone why he wants pleasure, it is only slightly less silly to ask someone why he is doing something which is obviously pleasant. "Why are you eating and drinking?" is not a question which often has to be asked. Consequently, the contexts in which "because I enjoy it" will occur in the way in which Nowell-Smith describes will be those in which the agent is doing something odd, e.g. masochistic. To approach the topic of pleasure via the notion of 'block-words' is therefore to take freak pleasures as the central cases, and to reverse the natural order of investigation.

Writing about the descriptive use of "pleasure" Nowell-Smith has this to say:

Words such as "pain" and "hurt" that are normally used with a con-force can also be used as generic expressions to refer to those sensations and bodily conditions to which most people normally have a con-attitude. They then become descriptive, and as far as I can see there is no reason why "enjoy" "detest" "like" and "dislike" should not go the same way.

This seems to suggest that sensations of pain are recognized quite independently of the 'attitude' which people have towards them. There is no need to insist again that the word "pain" could not acquire a sense by any process which made no reference to pain-behaviour. Still, there are cases where a man can quite intelligibly say that he feels a pain, and yet exhibit no pain-behaviour; and it is these cases which Nowell-Smith has in mind when he talks of "pain" being used purely descriptively. And parallel to these cases are the cases where "pleasure" occurs as part of the name of a sensation. It is possible to feel sexual pleasure and to want this sensation to stop; a man who in such a situation said "I feel pleasure" would in Nowell-Smith's terminology be using the word "pleasure" purely descriptively.

But Nowell-Smith's projected descriptive use of "enjoy" is not in the same case; if only because "enjoyment" unlike "pain" and "pleasure" is never the name of a sensation. Nowell-Smith argues for his position as follows:

It is sophisticated, but not logically impossible, to enjoy a painful sensation and to want to prolong it; there are no logical limits to the possibilities of masochistic enjoyment.

It is not clear whether this is meant to be an example of the descriptive use of "pain" or of "enjoy". The context would lead us to think the latter; but does not the fact that the man wants to prolong his pain show that his use of "I enjoy it" is not purely descriptive? If it is the descriptive use of "pain" that is being illustrated, then this does not help us to see how "enjoy" can be used descriptively to refer to a sensation. In any case, how are we to settle the following question: Does whipping cause the masochist a different sensation from the ordinary man, or does it cause him the same sensation which he, unlike the rest of us, happens to like? To this question one answer is as good as the other; which shows that there is no possibility of setting up criteria for the sameness of sensations independently of what causes them and what people do about them. The only reason why we call the masochist's sensation "pain" is that we know it was produced by whipping. Suppose that it was produced instead by stroking his hand. If he now says "Do go on, this pains me intensely" are we merely to say "Ah, I see he is using "pain" purely descriptively"?

I claimed earlier that there were some human actions

143

which were enjoyed unless something went wrong; cases where the *onus probandi* was on the side of unpleasure. These are precisely those actions which are done *for pleasure*. This sounds like a circular account: in order to show that it is not, I must now distinguish between two things which I have hitherto pretended were the same, viz. pleasure and enjoyment.

If an action is done for pleasure, then it is done for its own sake, with no ulterior motive or further end in view. In discussing motives, I outlined a pattern of human action which consisted in acting to secure the presence of some independently specifiable good or the absence of some independently specifiable evil. If a man perjures himself for money, then the receiving of the money is a quite separate event from the giving of the false evidence. When the charwoman scrubs the floor, then the previous dirtiness of the floor, and the subsequent cleanliness of the floor are both identifiable without reference to the charwoman's scrubbing. It would be foolish to raise the question whether the existence of a house was separate from, or identical with, the laying of its bricks and the fitting of its windows.

We saw also that there were some actions, such as those done for revenge or out of friendship, which did not in the same way produce some good for the agent specifiable independently of the action itself. Such actions, we suggested, were done in order to fulfil a specific pattern which, as a whole, served human happiness. There are other actions which produce no independently specifiable good for the agent, and which serve human happiness in themselves, and not merely as exemplifying a certain pattern. Such actions are actions done for pleasure. Typical examples are the taking of a holiday, the playing of a game, the pursuit of a hobby, the watching of a spectacle, the production of a work of art.

Doing a thing for pleasure is not the same as enjoying doing it. One can do something for pleasure and fail to enjoy it; and one can enjoy earning one's living. There is a sense of "enjoy" in which it is a sufficient condition for a man to enjoy ϕing that he should frequently ϕ for pleasure; if we know that a man frequently goes fishing without being forced to and without gaining anything by it, then we need no further information to decide that he enjoys fishing. But when he comes back from a particular day's fishing and we ask him: "Did you enjoy it?" we are not asking "Do you do this sort of thing frequently for pleasure?" It is in such a case that the 'unimpeded activity' view of enjoyment seems applicable. If the fisherman says "No, I did not enjoy it" we want to know what went wrong: was the weather unsuitable, were the fish too coy, did he have a headache or what? "The conditions were perfect, the fishing was excellent, and I felt in very good trim, but I didn't enjoy it" is quite unconvincing as it stands.

It now looks as if we could say: to enjoy ϕing (on a particular occasion) is simply to ϕ for pleasure successfully. In one sense this is true, and indeed truistic. The criterion for success in any activity is whether it achieves the goal at which it is aimed: so, just as if I write for money I am successful only if I make money, so also if I write for pleasure I am successful only if I enjoy writing. And so, in general, a criterion of success for recreational activities is pleasure: "I

145

had a good holiday, but I didn't enjoy it" is absurd; as is "It was a very bad party: we all found it extremely pleasant".

But if it is to be at all informative to say that to enjoy ϕing is to ϕ for pleasure successfully, then "to ϕ for pleasure successfully" must be taken not as "to ϕ for pleasure and to get pleasure" but as "to ϕ for pleasure and to succeed in ϕing". There must be some criterion for success in ϕing *other than* enjoyment if we are to explain enjoying ϕing in terms of ϕing successfully. But once we give such a criterion, then our account of enjoyment seems plainly false: one can enjoy painting a bad picture and derive pleasure from a game that one loses.

We are now fairly enmeshed in the embarrassment which beset Aristotle when, in the tenth book of the *Nicomachean Ethics*, he attempted to give an account of how pleasure was an *end* of activity. If we take the standard case of *end* as being a state of affairs brought about by the action which is a means to it, we must say that pleasure is like an end in being a reason for action and a criterion of success in action, and in not being a means to any further end; but that it is unlike an end in that it does not terminate action (one ceases to wash the dishes once they are clean; it would be absurd to cease potholing once it gave pleasure) in that it does not specify action ("washing" can be defined as "making clean", but "potholing" cannot be defined as "causing pleasure") and in that it cannot be identified separately from the action.

It was, I think, partly these points which Aristotle had in mind when he gave his notoriously obscure definition of pleasure: "Pleasure perfects operation

146

not as an inherent disposition, but as a supervenient end, like the bloom on the cheek of youth."[1] But the immediate context of this remark is a discussion of the pleasures of the senses, such as pleasant sights and sounds (1174 b 20–31); and though Aristotle clearly meant his account of pleasure to cover also pleasure in complicated activities such as playing a game[2] I think that it is only by considering simple pleasures of the sense that we can make anything of the account at all.

What, first of all, is the *energeia* which pleasure perfects? If I am correct in thinking that Aristotle is thinking of pleasures of the senses, the *energeia* will be, e.g., the taste of some pleasant dish. Now in the *de Anima* (425 b 27–426 a 28) Aristotle teaches that the *energeia* of an object of sense and the *energeia* of a sense-faculty are one and the same: thus, e.g., if a dish is sweet, then its tasting sweet to me and my tasting its sweetness are one and the same event. Of course a dish's *being sweet* is not the same as its tasting sweet to me; but, for Aristotle, being sweet is not an *energeia* but a *hexis*, which consists precisely in the ability to *taste* sweet. "*Sensus in actu*," said the scholastics, codifying Aristotle, "*est sensibile in actu*".

In the passage in the *Ethics* which immediately precedes the definition of pleasure, Aristotle has stated that both the sensible object and the sense-

---

[1] *N. Ethics* 1174 b 31. The points made above are all made by Aristotle in the passages preceding: pleasure is not an end-product (1174 b 14) nor the termination of an action which specifies it (1174 a 17–b 6); it is a ground of action (1172 b 9ff) and a 'perfection' (1174 b 14–20).

[2] Cf. 1175 b 12, on enjoying a play, and enjoying eating sweets in the theatre.

faculty 'perfect' this *energeia* (1174 b 24–25). Now the meaning of 'perfect' (τελειοῦν) is not here obvious: but from the use which Aristotle makes of the word throughout this context it appears to mean "to make something a (good) specimen of its kind".[1] This sense fits our present passage well: if there is something wrong with my faculty of taste (e.g. if I have a cold), or if what I am tasting is not sweet, or not particularly sweet, then the *energeia* will not be a good specimen of the kind "sweet taste".

Now pleasure, we are told, also perfects the *energeia*, but not in the same way as either the sense-faculty or the sensible object. A dish may not only taste sweet, but taste pleasant; just as a sunset may not only look red, but also look beautiful.[2] All that is necessary, Aristotle says, in order for the *energeia* of a sense to be pleasant, is that both the sense-faculty and the sensible object should be in the best possible shape.[3] Pleasure is therefore a supervenient quality which attaches to the *energeia* when the two elements whose union constitutes the *energeia* both possess all the qualities which they should.

The Greek word ἡδονή covers both "enjoyment"

[1] Cf. the frequent occurrence of such expressions as τελειοῦν τὸ εἶδος (1174 a 16, 18, 22, 28, b 6).

[2] I take it that the sweetness of a dish, and the redness of a sunset, are examples of the ἕξις ἐνυπάρχουσα with which Aristotle contrasts pleasure. I take it also that "the bloom on the cheek of youth" was meant merely as an example of something which as well as looking what it was, also looked beautiful; I suggest that Aristotle chose "those who have just grown up" (ἀκμαῖοι) as his example because this suggested the supervenience of beauty—at least to a Greek insensitive to beauty in children.

[3] "So long as what is perceived and what perceives are as they should be, there will always be pleasure in the operation of the senses" (1174 b 32–3; so also 1174 b 29–31).

and "pleasure" and it is clear that Aristotle's account
of pleasure meets exactly the same difficulty at this
point as our account of enjoyment met earlier. Either
the goodness of the sense-object in question *includes*
its being enjoyable, in which case nothing seems
explained; or else it can be independently specified,
in which case Aristotle's account seems false: the
most sensitive nose in the world put in front of the
most powerfully smelling manure in the world will not
necessarily find the experience pleasant.

The answer to this difficulty must, I think, be
sought along the following lines. There must be *some*
criterion of pleasantness for an experience independent
of whether it is *here and now* found pleasant. But there
need not be any criterion independent of what most,
or some specially qualified people, *in general*, find
pleasant. If we can assume some such criterion, then
Aristotle's point holds. If the wine is a good wine, then,
in the absence of special circumstances interfering
with enjoyment,[1] if you don't enjoy it, this shows a
lack of discrimination on your part; conversely, if a
man cannot tell claret from burgundy, then he cannot
particularly enjoy either.

But how is the criterion, e.g., for a good wine set up?
Only by what those with discriminating palates say
and do: those wines are good wines which they find
pleasant. In such fields, what the experts say goes.[2]
There is no circularity here; discrimination can be
tested quite independently from enjoyment, and

[1] Aristotle gives as examples of these being tired, bored, or careless
(1175 a 2–10).
[2] δοκεῖ δ᾿ ἐν ἅπασι τοῖς τοιούτοις εἶναι τὸ φαινόμενον τῷ σπουδαίῳ
(1176 a 16).

enjoyment in general can be tested independently of enjoyment on a particular occasion.

So also with recreations and the other enjoyments considered earlier. There are criteria for success for games, parties, and hobbies, independent of whether they are, on a particular occasion, enjoyed or not: a good game must be fairly evenly matched, at a good party the guests must mix, a hobby should not be too exacting nor too expensive and so forth.[1] These criteria are not independent of what people, in general, enjoy doing: i.e. of what games they will play without being paid to, what sort of parties they will attend when not forced to, what occupations they will take up in their spare time. But if, by these general criteria, an enjoyment is a successful one, then someone who engages in it must give a special reason for saying, on a particular occasion, that he did not enjoy it.

---

[1] Criteria for the success of an enjoyment are not the same as criteria for success *in* the activity which is done for pleasure; hence it is not necessary that one should *win* a game for it to be a good game, or that one should paint *good* pictures for painting to be a good hobby.

CHAPTER SEVEN

ACTIONS AND RELATIONS

THE description of human feeling and of human willing is dependent on the description of human action. Several of the philosophical errors already discussed sprang from failure to realize this fact. In order to complete our account of the emotions and to prepare for a theory of the will we must now enter upon an analysis of the concept of *action*.

Many philosophers have elucidated the concept of *substance* by examining the logical behaviour of the proper names and common nouns by which we refer to substances. Others have drawn helpful distinctions between different types of qualities and relations by discussing the adjectives and relational expressions which we use to talk about these matters. Few, by comparison, have tried to clarify the concept of *action* by considering the special logical properties of the finite verbs which we employ to report actions. This I shall now attempt to do.

I shall try to isolate a simple and fundamental pattern of description of human activity, which reports of emotional states and reports of voluntary action alike exemplify. I shall call this pattern the pattern of "act and object", and I shall explore its

151

properties in three stages. First, I shall make a distinction between actions and relations, and thus prepare the way for a logical distinction to correspond to the grammatical distinction between the subject and the object of a transitive verb. Secondly, I shall distinguish between verbs of various types, and shall single out one type as palmary for the description of voluntary action. Finally, I shall distinguish between various types of object; and armed with the distinctions thus made, I shall go on, in the last two chapters of the book, to offer a sketch of a theory of the will.

Logicians, like philosophers, have concerned themselves comparatively little with the expressions which describe human actions. Names, definite descriptions, predicates, and relational expressions have all been amply discussed; little special discussion has been devoted to verbs of action. If a verb of action is intransitive, like "doodles", it is treated as a one-place predicate, like ". . . is blue"; if transitive, like ". . . killed . . .", it is classed with dyadic relation expressions, such as ". . . is larger than . . ."; if it 'takes a dative', like ". . . gives . . . to . . ." it is put on a par with triadic relation expressions, such as ". . . is between . . . and . . .". As a corollary of this way of looking at things, the distinction sometimes made by grammarians between subject and object is treated as philosophically useless. It is clear off-hand that in "Peter is taller than Paul" "Peter" has no more and no less claim to be regarded as the subject of the sentence than "Paul"; it has been assumed similarly that there is no difference in status between "Peter" and "Paul" in "Peter ate Paul".

This treatment of verbs of action, which began

perhaps with Peirce, has become fairly general since Russell. Professor Prior, for example, writes thus of "Brutus killed Caesar".[1]

No doubt grammarians would have no hesitation in identifying the subject of this as "Brutus", dismissing "Caesar" as merely the "object"; and it is certainly true that the proposition is about Brutus, and that what it says of him is that he killed Caesar. But it is equally true that the proposition is about Caesar, saying of him that Brutus killed him. "Brutus" and "Caesar" are *both* of them "subjects" in the logical sense, and the predicate is the "dyadic" predicate "... killed ...".

To someone unschooled in logic it would appear that there was at least as much difference in type between "John is taller than Mary" and "Cesare poisoned Lucrezia" as there is between "John is taller than Mary" and "Peter is insane". Pre-Russellian subject-predicate logic ignored the distinction between the second of these pairs of statements; may there not be a distinction between the first pair which post-Russellian logic has tended to blur? Aristotle, as is well known, distinguished between the categories of ποίησις and πρός τι. Some at least of his criteria for this distinction are sufficiently formal to merit the attention of logicians; and the distinction is, as I hope to show, of importance for any philosophical account of the description of human actions.

There are many good reasons for classing together both sentences of the first pair. Each sentence contains two names, so that both "... is taller than ..." and "... poisoned ..." may be called dyadic predicates.

<hr>

[1] *Formal Logic*, 85.

"Peter is insane", on the other hand, contains only one name, so that ". . . is insane" is a monadic predicate. Again, both sentences admit a conversion which is impossible in the case of the third. We may say, instead of "John is taller than Mary" "Mary is less tall than John"; and "Lucrezia was poisoned by Cesare" instead of "Cesare poisoned Lucrezia"; but we cannot turn "Peter is insane" into any sentence in which "insane" appears as the grammatical subject.

For many logical purposes, such features are all we need to notice about a sentence. The convenience of treating all dyadic predicates alike is so great that there can be no question of denying its legitimacy. Equally it provides no reason why we should not investigate what differences there are between actions and relations; any more than the convenience for some purposes of subject-predicate logic was a reason against distinguishing between dyadic and monadic predicates.

I shall henceforth use only the expression "dyadic predicate" to refer either to verbs of action or relational expressions, and shall reserve "relational expression" for expressions in the Aristotelian category of πρός τι. By "a verb of action" I mean a verb which may occur as the main verb in the answer to a question of the form "What did A do?" I shall restrict myself to a consideration of transitive verbs of action, such as occur in the sentences "Brutus killed Caesar", "Wren built St Paul's", "Mary roasted the beef", and "Shaw admired Caesar". I shall contrast these with relations such as those of comparison (". . . is taller than . . .", ". . . is cleverer than . . .") those of space and time (". . . is on top of . . .", "is between . . . and . . .",

". . . preceded . . .") and those resulting from actions
(". . . is the father of . . .").

It has long been known that no relational analysis
is possible of sentences containing intensional objects.
A relation can hold only between two things which
exist; in any true sentence a relational expression, if
it occurs, must stand between two proper names with
bearers or between two non-vacuous descriptions. It
cannot be true that John is taller than the present
King of France; it may be true that he admires
Ossian. True, one may have a relation to something
which no longer exists, and two things need not exist
contemporaneously to stand in a relation to each
other. It may well be that I am fatter than my great-
grandfather, though he died before I was born. But
a verb such as "admire" may stand before a name
that never had a bearer at all. The Greeks worshipped
Zeus, though Zeus never was.

However, sentences containing psychological verbs
such as "admire" and "worship" form a sub-class
of sentences reporting actions; and it would be im-
proper to argue from a property of this class to a
general distinction between action and relation. For
the existence at some time of William and Harold is
a truth-condition for "William defeated Harold" no
less than for "William was more crafty than Harold".
And the problems which arise about "Socrates worshipped Aesculapius" arise about "Socrates was a
worshipper of Aesculapius" which *prima facie* at
least is a relational sentence.

But there are more general considerations which urge
us to make a distinction between actions and relations.

(*a*) If "Brutus killed Caesar" is taken as expressing

a dyadic relation between Brutus and Caesar, it is difficult to see how one can deduce from it "Caesar was killed". "Caesar was killed" is a complete sentence, exhibiting no 'unsaturatedness'; and it is not a relational sentence. But the logic books give us no rules by which we can pass from a dyadic relational proposition to a proposition made up of a single-place predicate and a name. From "Brutus was younger than Caesar" one cannot deduce any proposition about the same subject-matter in which one of the terms of the relation has disappeared. "Caesar was older than" makes no sense, and "Caesar was older" means something quite irrelevant.

In some cases, a similar point may be made without bringing in any reference to the passive voice. "Plato taught" is entailed by "Plato taught Aristotle". There is no sentence "Plato is cleverer" which is entailed by "Plato is cleverer than Aristotle"; nor does Plato's being cleverer than Aristotle entail his being clever. Again, a proposition is a function of its argument, but it is not a function. The distinction between action and relation is not, then, merely a distinction between the relation of passive to active and the relation of converse relation to relation.

Actions, we might say, exhibit a variable polyadicity which is foreign to relations. If this is correct, it is of great importance; for polyadicity is not an accidental property of a relational expression, but a part of its definition. It is of the essence of any relation that its polyadicity should be stable; no relation could be, say, indifferently dyadic or triadic.[1] If,

[1] Thus, e.g., Russell, in *An Inquiry into Meaning and Truth*: "We can distinguish proper names from other words by the fact that a

therefore, we are to class actions with relations, we must find some way of showing that the variability of their polyadicity is only apparent.

It might be said, for instance, that a sentence such as "Caesar was killed" is elliptical; it really means "Caesar was killed by something or other". Let us allow this for a moment. It still remains true that "Caesar was killed" does not leave the hearer gaping as "Abraham is as old as" does. If we are to call "Caesar was killed" elliptical, we must compare it with a relational sentence where one term is not omitted, but unspecified. If we do this, then "Caesar was killed" still does not seem similar to "Caesar preceded something or other"; the first sentence seems to give us substantial information about Caesar while the second does not. I learn nothing about Plato if I am told that he is larger than something, but not told what; it may be useful to know that Plato taught, even if one does not know whom he taught. So that even if "Plato taught" is elliptical, it need not be relational.

But why, in any case, are we to say that "Plato taught" is elliptical? If it is because it can be filled out by having the name of one of Plato's pupils attached to it, then we may say that "Plato taught Aristotle" is elliptical because it may have "at Athens" added to it, and that "Plato is older than Aristotle" is elliptical, because it may have "by forty years" added to it. There is no theoretical

proper name can occur in every form of atomic sentence, whereas a word which is not a proper name can occur in an atomic sentence which has the appropriate number of proper names" (p. 45). A sentence is atomic, in the *Inquiry*, if it contains no logical words or subordinate sentences.

limit to the amount of further information that can be packed into any given sentence by appropriate further specification.

Or are "Plato taught" and "Caesar was killed" elliptical because we know that if Plato taught, then he taught somebody, and if Caesar was killed, then he was killed by something? But we know equally well that if Plato taught and if Caesar was killed, then there was some place and some time at which these activities took place; for all that, we do not, and cannot if this objection is to be upheld, call "Plato taught Aristotle" and "Caesar was killed by Brutus" elliptical.

According to Russell, not only are sentences such as "Brutus killed Caesar" of relational *form*: they are actually disguised descriptions of relations. He writes:

Consider for a moment what happened when Brutus killed Caesar: a dagger moved swiftly from Brutus into Caesar. The abstract scheme is: "A moved from B to C" and the fact with which we are concerned is that this is different from "A moved from C to B". There were two events, one A-being-at-B, the other A-being-at-C, which we will name x and y respectively. If A moved from B to C, x preceded y; if A moved from C to B, y preceded x. Thus the ultimate source of the difference between "Brutus killed Caesar" and "Caesar killed Brutus" is the difference between "x precedes y" and "y precedes x" where x and y are events (*Inquiry*, 35–36).

This account can hardly have been meant to be more than schematic, since the movement of the knife is not a necessary condition of the truth of "Brutus killed Caesar" (since Brutus might have used poison) nor yet a sufficient condition (since Brutus might have been a surgeon). But the point which we have just been making can be used to show that even as a scheme Russell's account will not work. On this account, "Caesar killed" becomes "A moved from C to somewhere else", and "Caesar was killed" becomes "A moved from somewhere else to C". But "A's being somewhere else" is not the name of an event; so that we cannot say that the ultimate source of the difference between "Caesar killed" and "Caesar was killed" is the difference between "x precedes y" and "y precedes x" where x and y are events.

(b) The second difference between actions and relations is the reverse of the first one. A sentence reporting an action not only can be shorn of one of its terms without making nonsense; it can also have further terms added to it in various ways. In "Brutus killed Caesar in Pompey's theatre with a knife", ". . . killed . . ." does not express a tetradic relation holding between Brutus, Caesar, Pompey's theatre, and a knife. For if it does, then either the relation is a chameleon-like one which is now dyadic, now triadic, now tetradic; or it is a quite different relation from that which occurs in "Brutus killed Caesar", in which case it is hard to see how one can infer the shorter sentence from the longer.

It is not at all obvious how we are to deal with such cases. "Brutus killed Caesar with a knife" is certainly not a logical product of "Brutus killed Caesar" and any other proposition such as "Brutus used a knife". We might suggest, as before, that "Brutus killed Caesar" is, in fact, an abbreviation for "(Ex) (Brutus killed Caesar with an x)"; in that case the inference from "Brutus killed Caesar with a knife" to "Brutus killed Caesar" would be a simple case of existential generalization: ϕa only if $(Ex)\,(\phi x)$. But we meet with the same difficulty as before: what other circumstances are we to allow as lurking unspecified in the apparently simple "Brutus killed Caesar"?

There is a Latin tag which gives a far from exhaustive list of the questions which can be asked about the circumstances of any particular action: *"Quis? quid? ubi? quibus auxiliis? cur? quomodo? quando?"* If we answered all these questions, we might say that Brutus killed Caesar in Pompey's theatre with a knife out of jealousy clumsily on the Ides of March. In order, then, to safeguard the possibility of inferring from this that Brutus killed Caesar, we shall have to say that "Brutus killed Caesar" is an elliptical form of "$(Ez)(Ey)(Ex)(Ew)(Ev)$ (Brutus killed Caesar in v with a w out of x $y$ly on z)". Even so, we have obviously hardly begun. If we cast our net widely enough, we can make "Brutus killed Caesar" into a sentence which describes, with a certain lack of specification, the whole history of the world.

Following a suggestion of Professor Prior, we might deal with "Brutus killed Caesar with a knife" by treating "It was with a knife that . . ." as an operator which is prefixed to the sentence "Brutus killed Caesar"; let us abbreviate it to "$+$".[1] We can make it an axiom that $C+pp$, and thus safeguard the inference from "Brutus killed Caesar with a knife" to

[1] "It was not with a knife that . . ." cannot be rendered as "$N+$", because "It was not with a knife that Brutus killed Caesar" implies that Brutus killed Caesar just as "It was with a knife that Brutus killed Caesar" does. But if we have both "$CN+pp$" and "$C+pp$" we can prove anything whatever; for there is a thesis of the propositional calculus $CCNpqCCpqq$.

"Brutus killed Caesar". Again, there will be an *embarras de richesse*; we shall have an indefinite number of non-truth-functional operators on our hands. Moreover, such operators will not form significant sentences out of all sentences without distinction; and the differences between sentences such as "Brutus killed Caesar" and "Brutus was next to Caesar" will have to come out in the form of rules specifying which sentences admit of which operators. "It was with a knife that . . ." can be attached only to the first of these sentences, whereas "It was in the Forum that . . ." can be attached to both.[1]

But if "It was in the Forum that . . ." can be added to some relational sentences, how can I make the possibility of adding further terms to a sentence a ground for distinguishing between actions and relations? The distinction must be based, in fact, not on the mere possibility of introducing further terms into a sentence, but on the introduction of further terms which cannot be eliminated by the analysis of the lengthened sentence as a logical product of other sentences of stable polyadicity. "Brutus was next to Caesar in the Forum" has the same force as "For some time *t*, Brutus was in the Forum at *t*, Caesar was in the Forum at *t*, Brutus was next to Caesar at *t*". But "Brutus killed Caesar with a knife" has not the same force as "For some time *t*, Brutus killed Caesar at *t*, and Brutus used a knife at *t*". For perhaps Brutus with his left hand put poison in Caesar's cup while

[1] We may try to avoid this by laying down that wherever "*p*" is that sort of sentence to which "It was with a knife that . . ." cannot be significantly attached (e.g. "Brutus did not kill Caesar"), then " $+p$ " is to count as false. But difficulties then arise in applying the calculus.

with his right hand spinning a knife to determine which of the conspirators should reply to Mark Antony's forthcoming funeral oration.

With some exceptions to be considered later, it seems that spatio-temporal qualification can be applied indifferently to sentences reporting actions and sentences expressing relations. And it seems possible to deal with this sort of specification by one of the generalizing methods which we have just rejected for "with a knife". Prior, for example, has worked out systems for temporal specification in his book *Time and Modality*. The reason why such systems can be devised for space and time, but not for other additional elements in a sentence, seems to be that if a sentence is of a kind to which space-time specifications *can* be attached, then *some* such specification must be appropriate. Any event which has occurred at all must have occurred at some time and in some place. It is not similarly true that any action which could have been performed with an instrument *must* have been performed with some instrument, nor that any operation which could have been undertaken from a motive *must* have been undertaken from some motive. Hence, there is an artificiality in construing "Brutus killed Caesar" as (Ex) (Ey) (Brutus killed Caesar with an x out of y)" which there is not in construing it as "$(Es)(Et)$ (Brutus killed Caesar at s and t)".

(*c*) A third feature, akin to the two preceding ones, distinguishes action-sentences from relation-sentences. There is always more than one way in which a sentence containing a transitive verb of action may be false: there is not always more than one way in which a

162

relation-sentence may be false. In one sense, of course, *any* proposition may be false in indefinitely many ways; that is to say, any number of states of affairs may be described which would make it false. Thus "my watch is on the table" may be false either because my watch is on my wrist or because it is at the mender's.[1] A different sense of "being false in more than one way" is here in question. A sentence may be false in more than one way, in this sense, if and only if more than one state of affairs which would make it false may be described *merely by the use of terms occurring in the sentence itself* along with quantifiers, variables, and the negative operator.

Consider the sentence "Lear gave away his kingdom to Cordelia". Now this may be false either because Lear did not give his kingdom to anyone, or because it was not to Cordelia that he gave his kingdom, or because he did not give anything to Cordelia, or because it was not his kingdom which he gave to Cordelia, or because he did not give anything to anyone. That is to say, the truth of any of the following propositions is a sufficient, though not a necessary, condition of the truth of "Lear did not give his kingdom to Cordelia".

(1) Lear did not give his kingdom to anyone.
(2) It was not to Cordelia that Lear gave his kingdom.
(3) Lear did not give anything to Cordelia.
(4) It was not his kingdom that Lear gave to Cordelia.
(5) Lear did not give anything to anyone.

Given a finite number of objects which are Lear's to give away, and given a finite number of persons to

[1] Cf. Miss Anscombe, *An Introduction to Wittgenstein's Tractatus*, 34-35.

whom he may give them, all these sentences can be shown to be truth-functions of sentences of the form "Lear gave Cordelia his kingdom", though they are not truth-functions of this sentence itself, as "Lear did not give Cordelia his kingdom" is.

Suppose now that we try to construct a parallel set of ways in which the sentence "London is between New York and Moscow" can be false. We get the following sentences to parallel (1) = (5):

(i) London is not between New York and anywhere.
(ii) It is not Moscow that London is between New York and.
(iii) London is not between anywhere and Moscow.
(iv) It is not New York that London is between and Moscow.
(v) London is not between anywhere and anywhere.

These sentences are intuitively odd in a way in which (1)–(5) are not. The reason for this appears to be that (i), (iii), and (v) are false *a priori*; while (ii) and (iv) have no clear sense, and can be interpreted either so as to be not sufficient conditions for the truth of "London is not between New York and Moscow" or else as logical products of this and an *a priori* truth. For if London is something of which it is sensible to predicate *being between . . . and . . .*, then it must be between somewhere and somewhere. No parallel condition holds about predicating *giving . . . to . . .* of Lear.

(*d*) A different distinction between actions and relations is as follows. Where "ϕ" stands for a symmetrical relation, then given that "ϕab" is true, "ϕba" is true. *A fortiori*, if "ϕab" makes sense "ϕba" makes sense. Some relations are asymmetrical; even

ACTIONS AND RELATIONS

so, where "ϕ" stands for a genuine relation, then if
"ϕab" makes sense "ϕba" makes sense. If Cassius is
thinner than Brutus then Brutus is not thinner than
Cassius; none the less "Brutus is thinner than Cassius"
makes sense, and it is merely a contingent fact that it
is false. With actions such is not always the case. It
makes sense to say that Homer wrote the Iliad, but
not that the Iliad wrote Homer; "James wants a
holiday" if it is false, is contingently false; but it is
not a contingent fact that "a holiday wants James" is
false. If one were to treat *wanting* and *writing* as
relations, one would have to say that they were
asymmetrical not only with respect to truth, but also
with respect to meaningfulness. Let us call this
property of one-way meaningfulness "irreversibility":
a verb is irreversible if and only if there can be found
a significant sentence containing it (of the form subject-verb-object) which is no longer significant if the
subject and object are reversed. Irreversibility is a
property of psychological verbs generally,[1] but not
only of psychological verbs. Though "John ate James"
makes as good sense as "James ate John", "ate" is
irreversible by our definition, since "John ate a
cabbage" makes sense, whereas "A cabbage ate
John" does not. Not all verbs of action, however, are
irreversible. One can be pushed by anything which one
can push, and only what can defeat can be defeated.

This distinction is difficult to make precise, since the
notion of "making sense" is itself a vague one. Some
logicians might say that "a cabbage ate John" makes
perfect sense, though it has never in fact been true.
The type of nonsense which is produced by reversing an

[1] There are exceptions, e.g. "to feel friendship towards".

165

irreversible verb is akin to that which is given the equally vague name "a category mistake". One is indeed tempted to say that a relation must hold between entities of the same category, whereas there is no requirement of homogeneity between the subject and object of a verb expressing an action. Thus, one might contrast "Socrates is taller than virtue" with "Socrates pursued virtue", "John is twice the square root of two" with "John forgot the square root of two" and "Peter was underneath polio" with "Peter was killed by polio". But perhaps there is no absolute requirement of homogeneity between the terms of a relation. "Napoleon preceded the Peloponnesian War" makes sense, though *prima facie* Napoleon belongs to a different category from the Peloponnesian War.

Suppose that we were to draw up a list of all the terms with which a given noun can significantly occur in immediate conjunction. This list would contain expressions for properties, movements, actions, and relations. Thus, the list for "pebble" would contain such expressions as "... is black", "... rolled", "... crushed", "... is larger than". The lists for properties and movements would contain expressions for all and only those properties and movements which can be predicated of the given noun as subject. But when we come to the list of action-expressions, we shall have to make two separate lists, the first containing those expressions to which it can be joined as subject, the second containing those to which it can be joined as object. Thus, for "pebble" the second list would contain such words as "wanted", "saw", "recognized" which would not occur in the first list; because the expressions "... wanted a pebble",

". . . saw a pebble", "recognized a pebble" may occur in significant sentences, whereas "the pebble saw . . .", "the pebble recognized . . ." may not.

In the case of relational expressions, on the contrary, a single list will suffice, as in the case of expressions for properties and movements. Whatever is capable of occurring as the first term of a given n-adic relation is capable of occurring as the second or the nth term of the same relation. No distinction can be made between the various terms of a relation corresponding to that which can be made between the agent and the object of an action.

(5) We noticed earlier that psychological verbs could not be construed as relations because the object of a psychological verb, unlike the term of a relation, need never exist. There is a large class of non-psychological verbs which have a property partly analogous to this property of psychological verbs. I refer to verbs such as "make", "break", "create", "destroy", "eat", "beget". Such verbs are neither non-committal about the existence of their objects (like psychological verbs) nor do they presuppose it (like most relational expressions). Compare "De Gaulle is on top of the Eiffel Tower" with "De Gaulle is dreaming of the Eiffel Tower" and with "De Gaulle destroyed the Eiffel Tower". The first can now be true only if the Eiffel Tower now exists; the second can now be true whether or not the Eiffel Tower now exists; the third can now be true only if the Eiffel Tower does not now exist.

Relations such as " . . . is on top of . . ." demand the simultaneous existence of both their terms; relations such as ". . . is taller than . . ." demand only the existence at some time or other of both their terms;

actions such as ". . . makes . . ." demand the non-existence of their objects for all times prior to the action; actions such as ". . . breaks . . ." demand the non-existence of their objects for all times subsequent to the action; and actions such as ". . . admires . . ." do not demand the existence of their objects for any time at all.[1]

A relational analysis is as impossible for such a sentence as "Leonardo painted the Mona Lisa" as it is for "Socrates worshipped Aesculapius". For if "Leonardo painted the Mona Lisa" is true, it is not as if there were two entities, Leonardo and the Mona Lisa, between which a relation happens to hold. Did this 'relation' not hold, i.e. if Leonardo had not painted the Mona Lisa, then one of the terms of the 'relation' would not exist. A relational sentence is equally 'about' either of its terms. But regarded as a sentence about the Mona Lisa "Leonardo painted the Mona Lisa" seems to be a necessary proposition, since the Mona Lisa is essentially a painting of Leonardo's; regarded as a sentence about Leonardo, "Leonardo painted the Mona Lisa" is contingent, since Leonardo, while remaining Leonardo, might never have painted anything.

These considerations do not enable us to set up any further criterion for a general distinction between actions and relations. They merely bring out, by the consideration of one class of actions, the difficulty of extending a relational analysis to all verbs of action without exception.

---

[1] Relations such as ". . . wholly precedes . . ." are a special case. Like other relations, they *demand* the existence *at some time* of their terms; they *assert* their existence at a particular time.

It may be objected that precisely similar difficulties arise about certain relations. We have already suggested that whatever problems there are about "The Greeks worshipped Zeus" will arise about "The Greeks were worshippers of Zeus". Similarly, whatever problems arise about "Scott wrote Waverley" will arise about "Scott is the author of Waverley". Hence, whatever we are to say about these problems, they cannot be used as a wedge to thrust between relations and actions.

This objection is partly correct, but it calls not for the abandonment of our general distinction, but for the drawing of a new one. There is a large class of relations, such as *being the author of* and *being the father of*, which can hold between two terms only as the result of an action by one of the terms upon the other. It is because Scott wrote Waverley that he was the author of Waverley; it is because David begat Solomon that he was the father of Solomon; it is because John married Mary that he is the husband of Mary. Such relations generated by actions naturally share some of the properties of relations and some of the properties of actions. They are distinguished from the actions which generate them, as from many other relations, by their resistance to spatio-temporal qualifications. We can ask "When and where did David beget Solomon?" but not "When and where was David the father of Solomon?"

In this chapter I have tried to draw from various points of view a broad distinction between actions and relations. The distinction is not a sharp one, but has ragged edges: predicates which by some of the criteria suggested would count as actions would by others count as relations. Enough, I hope, has been said to mark the distance which separates the paradigmatic cases on either side, and to show that it is not to be taken for granted that the object of an action is simply the term of a relation. We must later distinguish from each other types of action so far treated together, and make more precise the notion of 'the object of an action'.

CHAPTER EIGHT

STATES, PERFORMANCES, ACTIVITIES

SO far I have not distinguished between various types of active verb which may be predicated of substances. I have spoken vaguely of "verbs of action", meaning verbs which may occur as the main verb in the answer to a question of the form "What did A do?" There are, however, many verbs which may be predicated of substances which do not fit this description; and among those which do, there are differences of type which are of philosophical importance. Such differences have often been neglected, because they become clear only upon consideration of the relations between the various tenses of the verbs in question; and tense-logic is a field which went almost unexplored between the Renaissance and very recent times.

No philosopher has paid more attention to the differences between verbs than Aristotle. The remarks that follow have been very largely inspired by passages in the *Metaphysics*, the *Physics* and the *Nicomachean Ethics*. However, the distinctions which Aristotle makes, and the criteria by which he makes them, cannot be simply carried over from Greek to English idiom. In order not to cumber the text with discussions of philology and exegesis, I shall not attempt to expound Aristotle's theses. Instead, I shall present a set of distinctions in their own right, and refer in footnotes to the passages in Aristotle which suggested them, without making any claim for exclusive authenticity of interpretation.

Let us first distinguish between those verbs which have, and those which have not, continuous tenses. In the second class fall "know", "be happy" and, in some uses, "see"; in the first fall "learn", "be cured" and "look for". We can say that a man is learning to swim, but not that he is knowing how to swim; that he was being cured, but not that he was being happy; that he will be looking for gold, but not that he will be seeing a joke. I shall call verbs of the second class "static verbs" and say that they stand for states.

The verbs of the first class must be subdivided into two further classes. For some of these verbs, any statement of the form "A is ϕing" implies a statement of the form "A has not ϕd"; for others it does not. For instance, if a man is building a house, he has not yet built it; if John is deciding whether to join the army, he has not yet decided to; if Mary is cutting the cake, she has not yet cut it. On the other hand, if I am living in Rome it does not follow that I have not lived in Rome; on the contrary, told that I am living in Rome you may at once ask me "And how long have you lived in Rome?" As with "live in Rome" so with "giggle", "listen to", "keep a secret", "ponder on": in all these cases, "A is ϕing" implies not "A has not ϕd" but rather "A has ϕd". Where "A is ϕing" implies "A has not ϕd" I shall call the verb a "performance-verb" and say that it stands for a performance; where "A is ϕing" implies rather "A has

ϕd" I shall call the verb an "activity-verb" and say that it stands for an activity. I shall continue to use "action" vaguely as before, to stand indifferently for a performance or an activity.[1]

Where "ϕ" is a static verb "A has ϕd" implies "A ϕs". We use such expressions as "I have loved her for seven years", or "I have been afraid of this all day" only when I still do love her or when I still am afraid. If I have ceased to do so, or to be so, then we most commonly use not the perfect but the simple preterite: "I loved her", "I was afraid of this". This implication from the perfect to the present does not hold where the verb in question is an activity verb. "I have acted foolishly" does not imply "I am acting foolishly". Nor, of course, does it exclude it. Whereas, where "ϕ" is a performance-verb, "A has ϕd" implies "A is not ϕing". If I have built my house, then I am not building it.[2]

[1] The difference between performances and activities may be brought out in another way. If "I am ϕing" is true at all times between 9 a.m. and 11 a.m. then it follows, if "ϕ" is an activity verb, that between 9 a.m. and 10 a.m. I ϕd. Not so with performance verbs. If I kept a secret from 9 until 11, then I kept a secret from 9 until 10 and so for any smaller period of time. But if "I am writing a sermon" is true at all times from 9 until 11, it does not follow that I wrote a sermon between 9 and 10. If I write a sermon between 9 and 11, then I write part of the sermon between 9 and 10; whereas, if I keep a secret from 9 until 11, I do not keep part of the secret from 9 until 10 and the other part from 10 to 11. (Cf. Aristotle, *N. Ethics*, 1174 a 21–29).

[2] Aristotle distinguishes between κινήσεις such as οἰκοδόμησις and μάθησις and ἐνέργειαι such as ὅρασις, εὐδαιμονία. Our performances correspond to Aristotle's κινήσεις and both states and activities to ἐνέργειαι (Metaphysics 1048 b 18–36). Elsewhere (e.g. *De An.* 417 a 30–b 2) Aristotle makes a distinction between ἔχειν and ἐνεργεῖν which corresponds to our distinction between state and activity; and in *N. Ethics*, 1140 a 1–24, between ποίησις and πρᾶξις which corresponds to our distinction between performance and activity.

It would be tedious to proceed further in the text with a comparison of the tense-implications of verbs of the three classes. They will be found summarised, with some unavoidable over-simplification, in the chart on the following page. The logical importance of them may be made clear in a single example. It is sometimes said by logicians that if a proposition is true now, then the corresponding past-tensed proposition will be true in the future: e.g. if "Mr Macmillan is Prime Minister" is true now, then "Mr Macmillan was Prime Minister" will be true in the future. This rule as it stands does not apply to performance-verbs. A man may be walking to the Rose and Crown, and yet never walk there, perhaps because he is run over on the way; and one can start knitting a sweater and end up by producing a scarf. Consequently, if "Alf is walking to the Rose and Crown" is now true, it does not follow that "Alf walked to the Rose and Crown" will be true; nor will "Mary knitted a sweater" be true merely because "Mary is knitting a sweater" is true. To be sure, if Mary is knitting a sweater, then it will be true that Mary *was knitting* a sweater, and we might say that the past tense which corresponds to "is knitting" is "was knitting" rather than "knitted". But if we say this, then we must make the same point in another way by saying that with performance verbs the past-tense which corresponds to the non-frequentative present is not the simple past tense.

In general, it is only once A has ϕd, that we can say that it will be true that A ϕd. It is therefore only when a present-tensed proposition contains a verb for which the inference from present to perfect holds that we can

Static Verbs	Performance Verbs	Activity Verbs
"A is φing" not used †	A is φing only if A has been φing	A is φing only if A has been φing
"A φs" not frequentative	"A φs" frequentative	"A φs" frequentative
A φs if A has φd	A φs only if A has φd; A has φd not only if A φs.	A φs only if A has φd; A has φd not only if A φs
	A is φing only if A has not φd	A is φing only if A has φd
	A was φing not only if A φd; A φd only if A was φing	A was φing if and only if A φd

Note † Many verbs for states have an idiomatic continuous present ("I am hoping", "I am intending"). These are not genuine continuous presents: for them, but not for true continuous presents, the rule holds "A is φing if and only if A φs".

Examples:

Static Verbs:	"understand", "know how", "love", "mean", "fear", "exist", "be able", "be blue", "perceive", "be taller than",
Performance Verbs:	"discover", "learn", "find", "kill", "convince", "grow up", "think out", "build a house", "wash", "cut", "lift", "decide whether",
Activity Verbs:	"listen to", "keep a secret", "weep", "laugh", "talk", "enjoy", "live at Rome", "stroke", "ponder on".

say that the corresponding simple-past-tensed proposition will be true. And the inference from present
to perfect holds only for certain states and activities,
not for performances.

Another difference between performance-verbs and
other verbs is that only performances take time. States
may *last for* a time, and activities *go on for* a time;
only performances *take* time. We may ask how long it
took to paint the door blue, but not how long it took
the door to be blue; it takes human beings twenty-one
years to become adults, but there is no time which it
takes them to be adults; thinking about a problem
does not take time as thinking it out does. One can
intend to do something for a long time, but one cannot
take a long time to intend it; one may giggle for five
minutes, but one does not take five minutes to giggle.
Performances are performed *in* a period of time;
states and activities are prolonged *for* a period of time.
We travel to Rome *in* three days, and stay there *for*
three days; if we spend an hour in a successful search
for the thimble, then we look for it *for* an hour and
find it *in* an hour.[1]

Because to do something quickly is to take a short
time to do it, and to do something slowly is to take
a long time to do it, only those actions which take
time can be done quickly or slowly. Static verbs and
activity-verbs cannot be qualified by these adverbs,
but only performance verbs. Mary may bake cakes
faster than Jane, but she cannot be beautiful faster

---

[1] Cf. Aristotle, *Nicomachean Ethics*, 1174 b 8: κινήσεις are
ἐν χρόνῳ unlike ἐνέργειαι. His point has sometimes been missed
by philosophers who have not noticed the difference between
taking time and *lasting for* a time.

than Jane; it is possible to learn French slowly, but
not to know French slowly. Of course, one can see
a joke quickly, just as one may take a long time to
see a joke, though seeing a joke is not a performance;
but this means merely that the time between hearing
and seeing was short or long, not that the seeing of
the joke was something which it took a shorter or
longer time to complete. Only performances can be
complete or incomplete. Contrast "I've not yet
finished drying the baby" with "I've not yet finished
loving the baby", and "I'm half-way through drinking
the whisky" with "I'm half-way through wanting a
drink". Activities and states may be prolonged indefinitely or they may cease; performances come to a
definite end and are finished. I can go on keeping a
secret for ever; I can only go on telling a secret until
it is told.[1]

Performances are brought to an end by states. Any
performance is describable in the form: "bringing it
about that p." Washing the dishes is bringing it
about that the dishes are clean; learning French is
bringing it about that I know French, walking to
Rome is bringing it about that I am in Rome. In all
these cases, what is brought about is, by our criteria, a
state: "is clean" "knows" "is in Rome" are all static
verbs. A performance may be brought about no less
than a state: if the policeman is forcing the prisoner
to walk to the police-station, then the policeman is
bringing it about that the prisoner is bringing it
about that he is in the police-station. Thus, in "bringing it about that p", "p" may contain a performance-

[1] Cf. Aristotle, *N. Ethics*, 1173 a 33 (faster and slower) and *Metaphysics*, Z 1048 b 19 (πράξεις ὧν ἐστι πέρας).

verb instead of a static verb. But every performance must be ultimately the bringing about of a state or of an activity; otherwise we could have an action which consisted merely in bringing it about that it was being brought about that it was being brought about that. . . . If the description of the action in this form is ever to be completed, it must contain either a perfective verb or an activity-verb. One performance differs from another in accordance with the differences between the states of affairs brought about: performances are specified by their ends.[1]

Some performances, for instance, are bringings-into-existence: building a house is bringing it about that a house exists. Others terminate existence: burning the gasworks is bringing it about that the gasworks does not exist. Others are alterations which consist in bringing it about that some substance possesses a property which it did not hitherto possess; as painting Lord Beaconsfield's statue scarlet is bringing it about that it is scarlet, when hitherto it was subfusc. Others merely bring about a change in place: putting the baby to bed brings it about that the baby is in bed. The substance which is changed by a performance may be the performer himself: when I grow up, learn to drive a car, join the Communist Party or commit suicide, the new states of affairs which I bring about are all states of myself.[2]

Only performance-verbs have a true passive voice. In common speech we distinguish between things

[1] Cf. Aristotle, *N. Ethics*, 1094 a 4; 1152 b 14, 23 (ἐνέργειαι not γενέσεις are τέλη) and 1174 a 13ff (on the specification of performances).

[2] Cf. Aristotle *Physics* Γ. 201 a 9ff: types of κίνησις: γένεσις ἀλλοίωσις, αὔξησις, φορά.

which we do, and things which happen to us. Among the things we do are boiling kettles, winning races, treading on people's toes, and voting for parliamentary candidates. Among the things which happen to us are getting sunburnt, being beaten at chess, having our ribs poked, being sentenced to six months without the option. In general, this distinction corresponds to the distinction between the active and the passive voice; but there are many exceptions. The passive voice is indeed almost exclusively reserved for recording things which happen to us; but there are many expressions involving the active voice—such as "making a mistake" "falling over" "missing the bus"—which seem to be concerned rather with things which happen to us than with the things which we do. And there are more than usually many borderline cases to blur the distinction. Still, the distinction is not without importance; we are praised and blamed for what we do, envied or pitied for what happens to us.

Now what A does is very often what happens to B. When Nero set fire to Rome, one same event was both Nero's arson and Rome's burning. The same event would appear both in a list of things which Nero did and in a list of things which happened to Rome. But "Nero committed arson" and "Rome was burnt" do not have the same meaning, though it is the same event which makes each of them true. No doubt the full description of any event of this kind would demand the mention of both agent and patient; but we still have two ways of reporting the same event ("A ϕd B" and "B was ϕd by A"), and it is indeed possible to regard the notion of "an event" as an abstraction from these two forms of expression, designed to enable us to consider an occurrence without commitment to a special interest in either A or B.[1]

The idiom of English, and of several other languages, connects an event more closely with the patient than with the agent. In general, if A φs B, then the φing is the φing of B, not of A. When Romulus killed Remus, the killing was the killing of Remus, not of Romulus; when the rain spoiled the crops, the spoiling was the spoiling of the crops, not of the rain. There is a good reason for this idiom, which we can see if we ask, regarding any action: what changes as a result of this action? Is it the agent or the patient: i.e. is it the subject or the object of the verb reporting the action? With an important exception, to be considered later, the answer is always: the object. When A φs B, it is essential that after this event B should have changed; it is not essential that A should have changed. The stove, after it has boiled the kettle, may look, feel, and behave exactly as it did before doing so; but the kettle cannot have been boiled by the stove unless it is warmer than it was when the process of boiling started. To find out whether you have washed the dishes, it is of little use to inspect you; whereas an examination of the dishes is always a help to settling the question, and may indeed settle it definitely, if they are still dirty. To be sure, there will very often be a change in the agent as a result of an action: when I have chopped down the oak-tree, I am usually hotter and stickier than when I started. But this is not essential to the truth of "I have cut down the oak" as it is essential to its truth that the oak should not

[1] Cf. Aristotle, *Physics* 202 a 14–b 22, on the relation between κίνησις, ποίησις and πάθησις.

be in the same condition as it was. If I am so strong or so skilful that I can chop down the oak without turning a hair, no matter; but no amount of strength or skill could make it true to say that I had cut down the oak-tree without denting its bark.

At this stage the reader may press for a definition of "change *in* a thing". For it seems reasonable to say that X changes if some proposition about X changes its truth value. And if this is so, then does not an agent change both during and after an action? For the proposition "John is chopping up wood' was untrue, and is true now that John is chopping up wood; so does not his action change him, no less than the wood?

In this minimal sense of "change", it is true that an action involves a change in the agent. But there is still a change which occurs in the patient which need not occur in the agent, namely, that *after* the action is over, the patient must have changed, but not necessarily the agent. Even so, there will still be a change in both agent and patient: namely, that of each of them, some past-tensed proposition which was untrue is now true ("John has chopped up the wood", "the wood has been chopped up"). But what is peculiar to the patient is that after the event its *present* state must be different from its state before the event. That is to say, after the event, there must be true of the patient, but not necessarily of the agent, some present-tensed proposition which was not true of it before the action took place.

The present-tensed proposition which is newly true of the patient is, of course, the proposition "*p*" which occurs in the description of the action in the form "bringing it about that *p*". So that when A ϕs B,

A brings it about that ϕB, and the ϕing is the ϕing of B. But where "ϕ" is not a performance-verb, or is a performance verb which is grammatically intransitive, then the ϕing is the ϕing of A. The life of Johnson is the life lived by Johnson, and the thoughts of Kierkegaard are the thoughts thought by Kierkegaard.[1]

We can now see better why it is a mistake to regard a sentence reporting a performance as being of the same logical form as a sentence expressing a relation. "John is taller than James" cannot be rewritten in the form "John is bringing it about that . . ." We can see too that there is after all a distinction of philosophical interest corresponding to the grammatical distinction between subject and object. In a sentence containing both a subject-expression and an object-expression, the object-expression stands for that which changes as a result of the performance reported by the sentence. The subject-expression stands for the agent or cause of this change.

States, performances, and activities are frequently related to each other in the following manner. Many of the states acquired by performances are capacities; and many activities are exercises of the capacities

[1] In *Met.* Z. 1050 a 30–b 2 Aristotle contrasts faculties whose exercise is productive with those whose exercise is not. Building, he says, is in what is built, weaving in what is woven, and in general change is in what is changed; but seeing is in the seer, thought in the thinker, and life in the liver. In the former cases the ἐνέργεια is in the patient, in the others it is in the agent. The ἐνέργεια is the state which results from the change: "is built" in "the house is built" is a static verb. This is concealed by the existence of the form "the house is being built"; but this sentence is not about the house, since there is not as yet, and may never be, any house for it to be about. So though "build (a house)" is a performance verb, "be built" is static. What is a κίνησις from the point of view of the subject is an ἐνέργεια of the object.

thus acquired. Thus, when I learn French, I bring it about that I know French, i.e. that I have the capacity to speak French; and speaking French is the activity which is the exercise of this capacity. Sweetening the tea is a performance which brings it about that the tea is sweet; and the state of being sweet is the capacity for tasting sweet, which is an activity.[1]

Performance-verbs play a fundamental part in the description of human actions. This may be brought out by making a twofold contrast between performances and states.

All performance-verbs have imperatives; no static verb has an imperative. Contrast "Decide whether you are coming or not!" with "Intend to come!"; "Wash yourself!" with "See the point of this joke!"; "Hit him!" with "Be very angry with him!" Now voluntary action is action which can be commanded; one can φ voluntarily only if one can φ when one is told to. (The boy who claims to be able to move his ears at will arouses our suspicion if, whenever asked to waggle them, he says he doesn't want to.) Only what can be commanded can be decided upon or form the immediate object of an intention.[2] Of course, people

---

[1] Cf. Aristotle, *De Anima*, 417 a 22–b 2. Aristotle here distinguishes between two senses of ἐνέργεια; one, which is equivalent to our "state" corresponds to Aristotle's use of ἕξις elsewhere; the other, which corresponds to our "activity" is elsewhere replaced by πρᾶξις. The scholastics tried to sort out Aristotle's inconsistency by using *actus primus* for ἐνέργεια in the first sense and *actus secundus* for the second.

[2] Intention cannot be commanded, and one cannot intend to intend; yet intention is voluntary. But since "to intend to . . ." must be filled out with another verb, this does not count against the contention that the role of performance-verbs is primary in the description of voluntary action.

are praised or blamed for being or not being in certain states, e.g., for not seeing what they ought to have seen, or for feeling distress over something trivial. But they can be praised or blamed for this only if they could have brought it about that they were not in the state in which they now are. And "to bring it about that ..." is a performance verb; and any performance can be commanded. A man may be praised or blamed only as a result of not doing an action of a kind which, when commanded, he can do, or which, when forbidden, he can refrain from.[1]

Secondly, performances, unlike states, have purposes. We can ask "Why did you arrive at three o'clock?", but not "For what purpose do you see this joke?" "Why do you love Anne?" asks for your reason for, not your purpose in, loving Anne.

In these respects some activities are like states, and some are like performances. We do not have a purpose in enjoying things, nor do we ask "with what intention do you weep?"; on the other hand, we look for things in order to find them and listen to them in order to hear them. Similarly, we can be commanded to think of a number or to act generously, though not to take pleasure in something or to laugh heartily at a certain joke. Just as performances are describable in the form "bringing it about that p ..." so many activities are describable as "attempting to bring it about that p ...". So, listening is attempting to hear, searching is attempting to find, treating is

---

[1] The qualifications "when commanded" "when forbidden" are necessary; there are many actions which human beings can do, but not when commanded; e.g. vomiting.

attempting to cure.[1] All these activity verbs have imperatives, and all such activities can have purposes.
An activity-verb such as "enjoy", which cannot be
rendered as "bringing it about that . . ." has no
imperative either. It is thus clear that the form of
description "A is bringing it about that p" is the
fundamental one for the description of voluntary
human action. We shall return to this point later.

To conclude the present chapter, I will make a
point about the possibility of formalizing tense-logic
which follows from the distinctions we have drawn.
A system of tense-logic such as that drawn up by
Prior in *Time and Modality* treats tense as an attribute
not of verbs but of propositions; tense is symbolized
by an operator on the proposition as a whole, such as
"It will be the case that . . ." Such a procedure greatly
facilitates the formalization of a large number of
inferences involving tense; but it is bound to leave out
of account just those logical distinctions which have
been occupying our attention. Since it operates with
only three tenses, instead of the larger number at the
disposal of natural languages such as Greek and
English, it cannot bring out such differences as that
between the continuous and non-continuous present,
nor between the imperfect and the perfect past tenses.
There is no way, for instance, of expressing in Prior's
system the inference, for performance-verbs, from "A
is ϕing" to "A has not ϕd". Since the tense is, in
effect, passed on from the main verb of the sentence to
the 'verb' of the operator, and since the verb ". . . is

---

[1] These are Ryle's task-verbs (*The Concept of Mind*, 149ff).
Ryle's achievement-verbs fall into all three of our categories—
"know" is a state, "cure" a performance, "keep a secret" an activity.

the case that . . ." is, by our criteria, a static verb, the result of Prior's system is to turn all verbs into static verbs. To point this out is not to disparage the usefulness of tense logics of this kind; it is merely to suggest that they fall short of formalizing all those aspects of tense which are of interest to philosophy.

CHAPTER NINE

OBJECTS

IN the first part of this book I spoke frequently of the 'object' of an emotion or desire, contrasting the object of such a mental attitude with its cause. In the last chapter I described the object of an action as being that which changes as a result of the action. It is clear that we have here two different senses of "object", or two different kinds of object. The objects of mental attitudes are sometimes called "intensional objects": let us call the object of an action which is not a mental act a "non-intensional object". We must now consider the relationships and the differences between intensional and non-intensional objects.

It will, I hope, have been clear to the reader throughout that when I speak of 'the object of an action' I do not mean to refer to the point of an action, or the purpose or objective with which someone acts. I have also tried to avoid using the word "object" in such a way that it is equivalent to "thing" or "substance", as when people speak of finding a strange object in the cupboard, or philosophers talk of objects in the external world. The sense of "object" which I have hitherto employed and wish now to discuss is one which derives from the grammatical notion of the *object* of a transitive verb. The object of fear is *what* is feared, the object of love is *what* is loved, the object of cutting is *what* is cut, the object of heating is *what* is heated. In discussing the nature of objects we are simply discussing the logical role of the object-expressions which complete the sense of intensional and non-intensional verbs.[1]

There was a scholastic adage: *Obiectum specificat actum*. There are two ways in which objects specify acts. First, and obviously, one and the same verb may be used to report quite different actions if its sense is completed with different object-expressions. Smoking a pipe differs from smoking a cigar, and killing mice is not the same thing as killing men. Verbs completed by object expressions describe species of the genus described by a verb alone: stealing silk handkerchiefs is one sort of stealing, and eating snails is one sort of eating. Some of these specific distinctions are more important than others; in different societies different distinctions play different roles. In most societies the difference between killing men and killing mice is clearly marked; in some eating pork is significantly different from eating lamb. Much of moral philosophy could be regarded as an attempt to discover or lay down which are the significant specific differences between human actions.[2]

[1] If this is clearly understood, there seems to be little danger, and great convenience, in talking of 'objects' rather than of 'object-expressions'. Geach criticizes this usage on the grounds that it leads to saying e.g. "some objects of mental acts do not exist". But this sentence is unobjectionable so long as it means only that some object expressions lack reference.

[2] For the scholastic dictum cf. Aquinas, *Summa Theologica* Ia 77, 3; and Ia IIae 18, 2: *actio habet speciem ex obiecto, sicut et motus ex termino*. The doctrine is based on passages in Aristotle, e.g. *De Anima* II 415 a 14ff, *N. Ethics*, 1174 b 5.

Objects specify acts in another way, which was brought out by the scholastic distinction between material and formal objects. Anything which can be ϕd is a material object of ϕing. Beer, for example can be seen, and so beer is a material object of seeing; when the executioners burnt Joan of Arc, Joan was the material object of their burning. The formal object of ϕing is the object under that description which *must* apply to it if it is to be possible to ϕ it. If only what is P can be ϕd, then "thing which is P" gives the formal object of ϕing. Descriptions of formal objects can be formed trivially simply by modalising the relevant verbs: only what is edible can be eaten, only what is inflammable can be burnt, only what is tangible can be touched. But there are other descriptions of formal objects which are not trivial in this way. Only what is dirty can be cleaned, only what is wet can be dried, only what is coloured can be seen, only what is criminal can be committed, only what is difficult to obtain can be striven for, only other people's property can be stolen. "Other people's property" is a description of the formal object of *stealing*, just as "one's own spouse" is a description of the formal object of *divorcing*. Joan of Arc was the formal object of burning not *qua* saint, nor *qua* woman, but *qua* inflammable material.

To assign a formal object to an action is to place restrictions on what may occur as the direct object of a verb describing the action. The restrictions may be of various kinds. They may, for example, concern time: only what is past can be remembered or avenged, only what has not yet happened can be dreaded or awaited. Or they may concern place: only what is present can be enjoyed, only what is absent can be missed. Or they may concern good and evil; only something thought to be good can be envied, only something thought to be evil can be regretted. There is no formal object of *thinking of*, because there are no restrictions on what may be thought of: any expression which can occur as an object-expression after any verb, can occur as an object-expression after the verb ". . . think of . . .". So that if we are to say that there is a formal object of thought we must say that it is: anything whatever.[1]

A formal object should not be confused with an internal accusative, such as occurs in the expressions "to dream a dream", "to play a game". The dream is not anything over and above the dreaming, nor the game over and above the playing; but my neighbour's property can be identified as such quite independently of my stealing it, and my wife is not brought into existence by my divorcing her.

Formal objects specify actions in a manner different from that in which, as we saw above, all objects specify actions. Verbal nouns, like other nouns, may be ordered in accordance with the scheme of genus and species: murder is one sort of homicide, and homicide is one sort of killing; spying is one sort of treason, and treason is one sort of crime. One way in which a species of action may be differentiated from other species of the same genus is by a difference in

---

[1] This is the meaning of the scholastic expression "*obiectum intellectus est ens ut sic*". This dictum is sometimes quaintly interpreted by neo-Scholastics as meaning that the intellect is a faculty for the intuition of Pure Being.

its formal object.[1] Thus, if we take (voluntary) killing as a genus, homicide differs from other species in this genus as being the killing of *a human being*; if we take homicide as a genus, murder differs from other species in this genus as being the killing of an *innocent* human being. If we take making as a genus, then cobbling differs from tailoring because the formal object of the one is footwear and of the other clothes.

Now both intensional and non-intensional actions are specified by their formal objects: this, and not the mere grammatical similarity between such sentences as "Macbeth feared Banquo" and "Macbeth killed Banquo", is the reason for treating intensional and non-intensional objects together before distinguishing between them. Emotional attitudes, like other mental attitudes, have formal objects; some of the philosophical errors about the emotions which we considered in the first part of this book might be described as mistakes about their formal objects. Descartès and Hume, with the philosophers and psychologists who followed them, treated the relationship between an emotion and its formal object, which is a logical one, as if it were a contingent matter of fact. If the emotions were internal impressions or behaviour patterns there would be no logical restrictions on the type of object which each emotion could have. It would be a mere matter of fact that people were not angered by being benefited, nor afraid of what they already know to have

[1] There are other ways: roasting and boiling are species of cooking, but their formal objects are the same. So too one can *crawl to* anywhere that one can *walk to*. The difference between species in such cases is made by the manner, and not by the object, of the action (Cf. Aristotle, *N. Ethics*, 1174 a 31).

191

happened; just as it is a mere matter of fact that most people are nauseated by slugs crawling from beneath an upturned stone and sneeze on getting pepper in their nostrils. There would be no more reason why, once in a while, a man might not be grateful for being harmed, or be proud of a defect, than there is why, once in a while, a man may not feel a sinking in the stomach while being complimented, or weep on the receipt of good news.

In fact, each of the emotions is appropriate—logically, and not just morally appropriate—only to certain restricted objects. One cannot be afraid of just anything, nor happy about anything whatsoever. If a man says that he is afraid of winning £10,000 in the pools, we want to ask him more: does he believe that money corrupts, or does he expect to lose his friends, or to be annoyed by begging letters, or what? If we can elicit from him only descriptions of the good aspects of the situation, then we cannot understand why he reports his emotion as fear and not as hope. Again, if a man says that he feels remorse for the actions of someone quite unconnected with him, or is envious of his own vices, we are at a loss to understand him.

It is, of course, quite possible for someone to be grateful for a physical injury, if he regards it as having done him some good; as members of the House of Lords frequently tell us that they are grateful to those who caned them at school. It is also possible to be proud of a vice or a crime or a defect, if one can represent it to oneself as a virtue or an achievement or an advantage: as Don Juan may boast of his prowess with women, or Topcliffe brag of his skill as a torturer,

or a beggar in a bazaar glory in the unsightliness of
his sores. What is not possible is to be grateful for, or
proud of, something which one regards as an evil
unmixed with good. Again, it is possible to be envious
of one's own fruit trees; but only if one mistakenly
believes that the land on which they stand is part of
one's neighbour's property; just as it is possible to
feel remorse for the failure of the crops in Vietnam
if one believes that it was due to the inadequacy of
one's own prayers. What is not possible is to envy
something which one believes to belong to oneself, or
to feel remorse for something in which one believes
one had no part.

The medieval schoolmen gave expression to restrictions such as those we have outlined by saying
that the formal object of fear was a future evil, of
envy another's good, of remorse one's own past sins.
In this they were following Aristotle, who gives, in
his *Rhetoric,* but without the terminology, a list of the
formal objects of the emotions. It is not, of course,
correct to say e.g. that the formal object of envy is
another's good *tout court*: one must say that it is
something *believed to* be good and *believed to* belong
to another, as our example above shows. Thus
Aristotle in defining anger says that it is a desire for
what appears to be revenge for *what appears to be* an
insult.[1] The description of the formal object of a
mental attitude such as an emotion, unlike a descrip-

---

[1] *Rhetoric,* 1378 a 30ff: ἔστω δὴ ὀργὴ ὄρεξις μετα λύπης τιμωρίας
φαινομένης διὰ φαινομένην ὀλιγωρίαν. "φαινομένον" occurs also
in the definitions of pity (1385 b 11) envy (1387 b 22) jealousy
(1388 a 31), etc. The attempt of Cope (*The Rhetoric of Aristotle,* II,
10) to interpret "φαινομένης" as "φανερᾶς" seems totally unnecessary.

tion of the formal object of a non-intensional action, must contain reference to belief. Only what is wet in fact can be dried; but something which is merely believed to be an insult may provoke anger.

So far I have used "intensional action" and "intensional object" simply as equivalent to "mental act" and "object of a mental act or attitude" without giving any criterion for distinguishing intensional objects from non-intensional objects. We might define intensionality heuristically as "the formal property which is peculiar to the description of psychological events and states". The attempt, then, to give a proper definition of intensionality will consist in an attempt to find what formal property, if any, belongs always and only to descriptions of psychological phenomena. It was thus, historically, that the notion of intensionality was introduced, or reintroduced, into philosophy by Brentano.

Looking for a property which would mark off psychical phenomena from physical phenomena, Brentano first considered and rejected the suggestion that the peculiarity of psychical phenomena was that they lacked extension. He then proposed a different criterion of distinction:

Every psychical phenomenon is characterized by what the medieval scholastics called the intensional (or mental) existence of an object, and what we, not quite unambiguously, would call "relation to a content" "object-directedness" or "immanent objectivity". ("Object" here does not mean reality.) Each such phenomenon contains in itself something as an object, though not each in the same manner. In imagination something is imagined, in judgement something is accepted or rejected, in love something is loved, in hatred something is hated, in desire something is desired and so forth.

This intensional existence is a property only of psychical phenomena; no physical phenomenon displays anything similar. And so we can define psychical phenomena by saying that they are those phenomena which contain an object intensionally (*Psychologie von Empirischen Standpunkt*, Book II, chapter, 1 section 5).

In reading this passage we feel a certain difficulty. It is true that where there is love then *something* is loved, if there is to be hatred then *something* must be hated; but is it not also true that if heating takes place then *something* is heated and if cutting takes place then *something* is cut? "Heat" and "cut" are not psychological verbs: how then can Brentano say that object-directedness is peculiar to psychological phenomena? He appears to have taken a feature common to all grammatically transitive verbs as being a peculiarity of psychological verbs.[1]

The answer to this difficulty becomes clear only if we refer to the scholastics from whom Brentano borrowed the notion of intensionality. It will be remembered that in the last chapter we defined the object of an action as that which was changed as the result of an action. This definition applies only to non-

---

[1] Husserl, in a passage which reads like a commentary on Brentano's text, seems to accept the conclusion that *any* action which has an object is intensional. He writes "Wir verstanden unter Intentionalität die Eigenheit von Erlebnissen, "bewusstsein *von* Etwas zu sein" ... ein Wahrnehmen ist Wahrnehmen von etwas, etwa einem Dinge; ein Urteilen ist Urteilen von einem Sachverhalt; ein Werten von einem Wertverhalt; ein Wünschen von einem Wunschverhalt usw. *Handeln geht auf Handlung, Tun auf Tat*, Lieben auf Geliebtes, sich Freuen auf Erfreuliches usw ..." (*Ideen*, 204; italics mine).

psychological actions; and the scholastics placed the intensionality of psychological actions precisely in the fact that they did not change their objects. If Peter has painted his house, then Peter's house must now be different from what it was before he painted it; but if Peter has looked at his house, it may now be exactly the same as it was before he looked at it. To find out whether the doctor has cured his patient, we must examine the patient; to find out whether the doctor has fallen in love with his patient, we must ask or observe the doctor. Where a non-psychological action brings about a change, the change is in the object and not, save *per accidens*, in the subject; where a psychological action brings about a change, the change is in the subject and not, save *per accidens*, in the object.

Aquinas frequently makes this distinction between two different kinds of action: *actio manens in agente* and *actio transiens in obiectum*. Thus he writes:

There are actions of two kinds: some actions, such as heating and cutting, pass over into external matter; others, such as understanding, perceiving, and wanting, remain in the agent. The difference between them is this: actions of the first kind bring about a state not of the agent which initiates the change, but of what is changed; whereas actions of the second kind bring about a state of the agent.[1]

---

[1] *Duplex est actio: una, quae transit in exteriorem materiam, ut calefacere et secare; alia, quae manet in agente, ut intelligere, sentire et velle. Quarum haec est differentia: quia prima actio non est perfectio agentis quod movet, sed ipsius moti; secunda autem actio est perfectio agentis* (*Summa Theologica* Ia, 18, 3 ad 1; cf. also Ia 23, 2 1 & ad 1; Ia 34, 3 ad 2; Ia 37, 1 ad 2; Ia 54, 1 ad 3, etc.). Aquinas goes on to explain how the sense of "change" differs when we talk of the

This distinction solves the difficulty which we felt about Brentano's account of intensionality: but it presents difficulties of its own. The physician may heal himself, and the change thus brought about is in the agent; yet healing is not a psychological perform-ance, since drugs can do it as well as men. This difficulty, though of venerable antiquity, is fairly trivial; a more serious one concerns local motion. When I climb the Matterhorn, the change brought about appears to be in me: I who was at the bottom of the mountain am now at the top. But "climb" is not, or not obviously, a psychological verb. In this case, the change brought about is a change in the *relation* between myself and the Matterhorn: the state which ensues upon my action is expressed by the relational proposition "I am on top of the Matterhorn". And we have all along admitted, in company with most logicians, that in a genuinely relational pro-position both terms are on an equal footing. The result of the action has therefore no more claim to be regarded as a fact about the agent than as a fact about the object.

In our time, Brentano's thesis has been developed by Chisholm (*Perceiving*, Ch. XI). Chisholm gives three criteria for intensionality. The first is this:

A simple declarative sentence is intensional if it uses a substantival expression—a name or a discription—in

agent as changing from when we talk of the object as changing. My translation of "*perfectio*" as "*bringing about* a state" may be questioned; it was suggested by the parallel passage in Ia 87, 3c where *aedificatio* (a performance and not a state in the sense defined in the previous chapter) is called a "*perfectio*". Aquinas claims, perhaps without justification, to base his distinction on that made by Aristotle in *Metaphysics* Θ (1058 a 3–37).

such a way that neither the sentence nor its contradictory implies either that there is or that there isn't anything to which the substantival expression truly applies.

By this criterion, he observes, "Diogenes looked for an honest man" is intensional, whereas "Diogenes sat in his tub" is not.

Another criterion which Chisholm offers concerns what Quine calls "referential opacity". It may be summarized as follows. Let E be a sentence of the form "A=B" (where A and B are names). Then if P is a sentence containing A, and Q is a sentence like P except that it contains B wherever P contains A, P is intensional if P and E do not together imply Q. These are the criteria which Chisholm gives for diagnosing intensionality in sentences which do not contain propositional clauses.

An objection to these criteria is that by them many expressions containing psychological verbs are not intensional. "Know", for instance, is a psychologica verb, but "Diogenes knows an honest man" implies that there is an honest man; and "Dr Jekyll = Mr Hyde" and "James knows Dr Jekyll" together imply "James knows Mr Hyde", though of course they do not imply "James knows that Dr Jekyll is Mr Hyde". So far as I can see these criteria as they stand are sufficient, but not necessary, conditions for intensionality. The scholastic criterion therefore seems preferable for diagnosing the intensionality of a verb which is followed by a direct object which is a substantival expression.

Psychological verbs occur not only in sentences of the simple subject-verb-object form, but also, and most characteristically, in sentences containing *that-*

clauses. Examples are "think", "say", "wish", "decide", and "regret". Such verbs, obviously, need not be followed by *that*-clauses in all their uses: many take an accusative and an infinitive, or simply an infinitive, where the accusative in question would be the same as the subject of the main verb. Other psychological verbs, such as "want", "intend", and "urge", show a marked preference for these latter forms. We can say that it is characteristic of many psychological verbs that they occur in sentences which, though not containing any truth-functional connectives, contain more than one verb. Thus Russell classed reports of beliefs, desires and so forth under the heading "propositions with more than one verb".[1] We might take the possibility of occurring as the main verb of such a sentence as a criterion of intensionality.

However, among sentences which contain more than one verb we must distinguish between those in which one of the verbs is exponible and those where neither is exponible. "John began to smoke" differs from "John wanted to smoke" because the former sentence, unlike the latter, could be expanded into a compound sentence which contained no other verb but "smoke" and included expressions indicating times. Verbs such as "cease", "continue", "make a practice of", "repeat", "anticipate", though they all need to have their sense completed by the addition of a further verb, are all exponible no less than "begin". Thus, for example, when we say that Amundsen anticipated Scott in reaching the Pole, we may mean no more than that Amundsen reached the Pole before Scott did. Such verbs, when so used, are not intensional verbs.

[1] *Logic and Knowledge*, 216ff.

But besides psychological verbs and exponible verbs, there are other verbs which need completion by a second verb. Such are "help", "hinder", "imitate", "attempt", "avoid". One can help one's friends only by helping them to *do* something, and one can imitate one's boss only by imitating him *doing* something. There is no form of behaviour which is called "imitating" or "helping"; what counts as helping John or imitating James depends on what John is doing or on what James does. These verbs are not exponible: it is not sufficient for A to be helping B simply that the actions of A and B should between them produce a common result, nor is C imitating D merely because he is doing what D does. One raindrop does not help another to wet the lawn, and waves following waves upon the seashore are not imitating their predecessors.

However, these verbs do not form a separate class of intensional verbs over and above the psychological verbs. If we ask what must be true for John to be helping Mary to wash the dishes, besides the fact that both John and Mary are washing the dishes, we shall find ourselves having to mention such circumstances as that John *knows* that Mary is washing the dishes. If we ask what must be true of James to make it the case that he has avoided meeting Nigel, besides his not having met Nigel, we shall have to say that he did not *want* to meet Nigel. Verbs such as "assist" and "avoid" are non-exponible only because of their psychological content.

The verb "to be able", however, is neither exponible nor psychological and yet it needs completion by another verb: modal propositions are members of the class of propositions with more than one verb. Another non-exponible, non-psychological verb is "to bring it about that". We cannot, therefore, use the two-verb criterion by itself as a mark of intensionality.

Chisholm offers another criterion of intensionality which is of assistance here. He says that any non-compound sentence Q which contains a propositional clause P is intensional provided that neither Q nor not-Q imply either P or not-P. By this criterion "it can be the case that p" is not intensional, even though "it can be the case that . . ." is not a truth-functional operator; for "it cannot be the case that p" implies "not-p". But once again, Chisholm has given us a sufficient, but not a necessary, condition of intensionality. By this criterion "John knows that Queen Anne is dead" is not intensional, since it implies "Queen Anne is dead".

Chisholm's earlier criterion, of referential opacity, though it was inadequate as a diagnostic of intensionality in simple subject-verb-object sentences, serves its purpose well here. If Tully = Cicero, then if it is possible that Tully will rise from the dead, it is possible that Cicero will rise from the dead; similarly, if the medium is bringing it about that Tully will attend the seance, she is bringing it about that Cicero will attend the seance. So the criterion rules out "it can be the case that" and "is bringing it about that" but does not, as the other did, exclude "knows". For if John knows that Cicero was murdered it does not follow that he knows that Tully was murdered.

By these criteria of intensionality which we have borrowed from the scholastics and from Chisholm, reports of emotional states and acts of the will are intensional sentences. A consideration of the emotions and the will must therefore include an account of how such sentences containing intensional objects are to be analysed. To this the remainder of the book will be devoted.

CHAPTER TEN

JUDGING AND WILLING

THE most satisfactory analysis of intensional sentences so far put forward is the theory of judgement presented by Geach in his book *Mental Acts*. The theory is based on the analogy between judging and saying. Geach presents it in two stages: in section 14 he presents a revised version of Russell's theory of judgement; in section 18 he offers an analysis of the act of judgement in terms of *oratio recta*; and in section 22 he welds these two accounts into a single theory.

The theory of section 14 makes use of two technical devices. The first is an undefined non-extensional operator "Z", which operates upon a predicate to form out of it a new predicate of the same polyadicity. The second is the notion of 'an Idea' which Geach defines as the exercise of a concept in judgement. (Geach uses the word "concept" in such a way that it is a sufficient, though not a necessary, condition of a man's having a concept of *so-and-so* that he should have mastered the intelligent use of the word for so-and-so in some language. *Op. cit.*, 12–15). The theory put forward with the aid of these devices is that a judgement to the effect that things stand in an

n-termed relation ϕ itself consists of Ideas standing in the relation $Z\phi$. Thus, if b' is A's Idea of b, and c' is A's Idea of c, then "A judges that ϕbc" is to be analysed as "$(Z\phi)b'c'$." When James judges that blood is thicker than water, then James's Idea of *blood* stands in the relation Z (thicker than) to James's Idea of *water*.

In section 18 Geach draws attention to the possibility of reporting a man's thoughts by the metaphorical use of *oratio recta*, as in the Biblical expression: "The fool hath said in his heart "There is no God"." He puts forward and defends the suggestion that in every case it is possible to translate a report of a judgement into just such a report of a mental utterance of a quoted expression.[1]

In section 22 Geach combines the two accounts by offering an interpretation of the first in terms of the second. An Idea is interpreted as a mental utterance: James's Idea of *blood* is his mental utterance of "blood"; that is to say, it consists in his saying-in-his-heart something to the same effect as "blood". It follows from what has been laid down that the relation Z (thicker than) is the relation in which James's mental utterance of "blood" stands to James's mental utterance of "water" whenever James mentally utters "blood is thicker than water". What is this relation?

Any physical occurrence of the expression "blood is thicker than water" consists of the utterance by one

[1] This construction is an alternative way of reporting, not an explanation of, a judgement. For A to say in his heart that p it is neither necessary nor sufficient that he should rehearse to himself in imagination some sentence meaning that p.

and the same person of "blood" followed by "is" followed by "thicker than" followed by "water". Let us use, as an abbreviation for the description of the relation in which the expression "blood" then stands to the expression "water", the expression "Y (thicker than)". We may then illustrate the relation Z (thicker than) by saying that James's Idea of *blood* stands in the relation Z (thicker than) to his Idea of *water* if and only if he mentally utters an expression, any physical occurrence of which consists in the expression "blood" standing in the relation Y (thicker than) to the expression "water". Thus Geach's two theories are combined into a single theory.[1]

[1] My account is simpler than Geach's own, which seems to contain an unnecessary complication. On p. 100 Geach looks for a relation Y (sharper than) which will fulfil the following condition: when Smith's judgement consists of an Idea *a'* in the relation Z(sharper than) to an Idea *b'*, then there are expressions A,B,C, such that *a'*, *b'* are Smith's mental utterances of A, B, respectively, and Smith's judgement as a whole is a mental utterance of C, and any (physical) occurrence of C consists of an occurrence of A in the relation Y (sharper than) to an occurrence of B. He does not define "Y (sharper than)" as I defined "Y (thicker than)" but offers as an approximation to such a definition a definition of another relational expression "X (sharper than)" which runs thus: *d* is in the relation X (sharper than) to *e* if and only if *d* and *e* are utterances of the same person, and there are expressions D and E such that *d* is the utterance of D and *e* of E in that person's utterance *either* of D followed by "is" followed by "sharper than" followed by E *or* of E followed by "is conversely" followed by "sharper than" followed by D. Geach introduces this complication presumably because saying-in-one's-heart "some knife is sharper than some spoon" is the very same thing as saying-in-one's heart "some spoon is conversely sharper than some knife". But C is an expression, not a mental utterance; and the expression "some knife is sharper than some spoon" is not the same expression as "some spoon is conversely sharper than some knife". The difficulty in question is already taken care of by the definition of "mental utterance of" as "saying in one's heart something *to the same effect as*"; and if it were not, it would not be taken

I propose to inquire whether Geach's theory can be extended or modified to apply to affective psychological verbs as well as to cognitive ones, to apply to acts of the will as well as to acts of the intellect. It is obvious that any theory of judgement, if it works at all, must apply, at least in a modified form, not only to reports containing the expression "judges that" but also to reports containing such expressions as "believes that", "knows that" and "is doubtful whether". I wish to inquire whether this particular theory of judgement has any application to a different set of reports: those which contain such expressions as "wants", "is pleased that", "wishes that", "regrets that".

There are several reasons for expecting the theory to cover such cases.

(a) We have already seen that the object of a desire displays the same sort of complexity as the object of an act of judgement. "A wants X" does not report a relation between A and some entity wanted. *Wanting* X is always *wanting to get* X; and a description of *getting* X describes a state of affairs and not a thing

---

care of by Geach's complication either. For saying-in-one's-heart "some knife is sharper than some spoon" is the very same thing as saying-in-one's-heart "it is not the case that no knife is sharper than some spoon"; but no physical occurrence of this expression consists of an occurrence of "some knife" standing in the relation X (sharper than) to an occurrence of "some spoon". The condition to be fulfilled by the relation Y (sharper than) demands only that there should be *an* expression C, of which Smith's judgement is a mental utterance, which, if physically uttered involves the relation Y (sharper than); not that *any* expression of which Smith's judgement is a mental utterance should involve this relation. In fact, a mental utterance of any sentence will be a mental utterance of an unlimited number of equivalent sentences; a mental utterance of "p" will be a mental utterance also of "NNp" and of "NNNNp" and so on.

(Cf. above, p. 126). We might therefore expect that an analysis of a report of a desire should display the same structure as the analysis of a report of judgement.

(*b*) Geach introduces his analogy theory of judgement by pointing out that there are many languages in which, as in English, the only difference between the statements "James said that *p*" and "James judged that *p*" is that they have different main verbs. It is no less true that wherever, for example, we have a sentence of the form "James regretted that *p*" we may construct a sentence "James said that *p*" which will differ from it only in its main verb. But more important than such an analogy between a report of an emotion and a report of a statement is the analogy between reports of desires and reports of commands or wishes.[1] Just as there is no difference, except in the main verb, between "James stated that John married Mary" and "James judged that John married Mary", so there is no difference, except in the main verb, between "James commanded John to marry Mary" and "James wanted John to marry Mary". The Bible used the saying-in-the-heart construction to introduce commands no less than statements: one of the examples cited by Geach is "They said in their heart "Let us destroy them together"." Just as it seems that we could always report judgements by means of reports using *oratio recta*, so it seems that we could always report desires by using quoted commands or wishes.[2] Thus, the Kaiser's desire that God should

[1] "Wish" in English may mean either a desire or the verbal expression of a desire. For clarity's sake I shall use the word to mean only the verbal expression, e.g. a sentence in the optative mood.

[2] The suggestion is Wittgenstein's (*Philosophical Investigations*, I, 657).

punish England could be reported by the words "The Kaiser said in his heart "*Gott strafe England*"," just as Genesis reports God's willing that light should exist in the words "God said "Let there be light"."

(*c*) The entities involved in Geach's theory of judgement are 'Ideas' which he defines as "the exercises of concepts in judgements". Some concepts, and those the most important, are abilities to use words in a language; and the ability to use a word in a language includes the ability to frame judgements, in the expression of which the word occurs. But Geach seems to me to have gone wrong when he says that such a concept *is* this ability (*Op. cit.*, 53); for to have mastered the use of a word involves being able to use and understand it not only in statements but also in commands and wishes. In practice at least both uses are mastered together: we do not have occasion to say that a child has learnt the use of "horse" in statements, but not in commands; or that he can understand the indicative forms of "go" but not the imperative forms. Even in theory, the two uses of words seem to be exercises of a single indivisible skill.[1]

[1] If we have any doubt about this, it is because it seems possible that an understanding of commands might be present without an understanding of statements, rather than that the opposite state of affairs might hold. It seems just possible to conceive that a race of helots, whose tongues were cut out at birth, and who were spoken to only in imperatives, might be taught, by reward and punishment, to understand and execute the commands addressed to them. It does not seem possible to imagine a similarly dumb race who were spoken to only in the indicative: for how could their behaviour show that they understood the statements made to them? *Ex hypothesi* we can set them no tasks and ask them no questions. But could they not make use of the information we give them in pursuing their own tasks and satisfying their own desires? Perhaps so; but lacking linguistic means of expressing desire, they can have only

There seems, then, to be no reason in the nature of Ideas why they should not enter into relations with each other to form desires as, on Geach's theory, they enter into relations with each other to form judgements.

In the light of these considerations, it might seem that we could make a simple adaptation of Geach's theory to the field of desire. Let us attempt such an adaptation by making two alterations in the theory as stated. First, the notion of 'an Idea' must be extended, so that it is to mean: the exercise of a concept *either* in a judgement, *or* in a desire.[1] Secondly, we must introduce a new operator "W", of the same logical type as "Z", which is to be interpreted by reference to the verbal expression of desires in wishes and commands, as "Z" was interpreted by reference to the verbal expression of judgements in statements. Thus "The Kaiser wanted God to punish England" will be analysed as "The Kaiser said in his heart "God punish England!" "; both statements report a desire of the Kaiser's which will consist in his Idea of *God* standing in the relation W(punish) to his Idea of *England*. And we may go on to elucidate the relation W(punish) by means of an account of a relation V(punish) in which

[1] For the concept of *a* to be exercised in a desire it is not necessary that a word for *a* in any language should come before the agent's mind. A man who fumbles in his pocket for a shilling exercises the concept of *shilling* no matter whether he rehearses the word "shilling" in his imagination or not.

such wants as animals have; our utterances would therefore play a part in their lives so different from that which they play in our own that we could not describe their reaction to them as genuine understanding. It is significant that when we speak of animals "understanding" bits of our language, it is usually their reaction to our *commands* that we have in mind—we think of a dog begging when told to, or ceasing to maul an intruder when called off, and similar cases.

the expression "God" stands to the expression "England" in any physical occurrence of the expression "God punish England!"

We shall soon see that this account will not stand without modification. But before exploring its drawbacks, let us mention some of its advantages.

A propos of judgements, Geach remarks:

Given a statement made by James in a language L, the grammatical rules of L generally allow us to construct a piece of *oratio obliqua* that preserves the gist of the statement. ... Having done this, we need only tack on the expression in L for "James judged (that ...)" and we have a report in L of the judgement expressed in James's original statement. Moreover, if we have sufficient mastery of L to understand both the expression for "James judged (that ...)" and the piece of *oratio obliqua*, we shall understand the report so constructed, no matter what the actual sense of the remark done into *oratio obliqua* may be (*Op. cit.*, 10).

Geach observes that these simple facts impose severe logical restrictions upon analyses of judgements. One is that any such analysis must apply no matter what the logical structure of the clause which expresses what is judged. Another is that the analysis must preserve the 'sense' or 'direction' of any relation which enters into what is judged: must allow us to distinguish, that is to say, between the judgement *that ϕab* and the judgement *that ϕba*. Russell's theory of judgement, for instance, is defective on both these counts (*Op. cit.*, 47ff).

The paragraph quoted above remains true of English and of some other languages if throughout we substitute for the word "statement" the word "command"

and for "judged" and "judgement" the words "desired" and "desire" respectively. Suppose that a general issues the command "Let the cavalry advance!" We may render this into reported speech in two ways in English: we may say either "The general commanded the cavalry to advance" or "The general commanded that the cavalry should advance". To either "... the cavalry to advance" or "that the cavalry should advance" we may prefix "The general desired..." to obtain a report of the general's desires.

It follows that any analysis of desires must conform to conditions analogous to those which Geach points out for analyses of judgements. It is easily shown that our theory as so far stated conforms to these conditions. The difference between the Chancellor's desiring that coal should be cheaper than oil, and his desiring that oil should be cheaper than coal, is the difference between his Idea of *coal* standing in the relation W(cheaper than) to his Idea of *oil*, and his Idea of *oil* standing in the relation W(cheaper than) to his Idea of *coal*. Again, our analysis can be easily adapted to desires involving predicates of any polyadicity. Lear's desire which was a mental utterance of "Winds, blow!" consisted of the predicate W(blow) holding of Lear's Idea of *winds*. A desire to the effect that a three-termed relation ϕ should hold will consist in a man's having Ideas a' b' c' such that W(ϕ) a' b' c'. For "W(blow)" is a monadic predicate like "blow", and where "ϕ" stands for a three-termed relation, then so does "W(ϕ)".

Any modification which we find necessary to make to our theory must preserve these characteristics intact.

CHAPTER ELEVEN

SKETCH OF A THEORY OF VOLITION

IN this last chapter I shall consider three objections to the draft theory put forward. The first I shall discuss and dismiss. The second will lead us to modify both our own theory of volition and Geach's theory of judgement, while preserving the parallelism between the theories. The third will lead us to abandon the parallel, and to point out the difference between the intensionality of an object of willing and the intensionality of an object of thought.

The first objection may be put forward as follows.

Given a piece of *oratio obliqua* corresponding to a statement, we can always tack on "James judged that . . ." and "James believed that . . ." to it to make it a report of a judgement or a belief, no matter what the tense of the sentence done into *oratio obliqua*, and no matter what the opinion of the reporter concerning the truth-value of that sentence. The same is true of some affective verbs such as "hope" and "regret". But it is not in general true of affective verbs that they can occur with *that*-clauses of all tenses and without commitment about truth-value. "James feels remorse that . . ." cannot be followed by an *oratio obliqua* form of a future tensed sentence, and "James wants that . . ." cannot be followed by a verb in the past tense, or in any tense in the indicative mood. Indeed, for many affective verbs, the natural construction in English is not a *that*-clause at all.

Instead of the simple parallel between judging and stating, we have a bewildering array of affective verbs followed by different constructions and with different restrictions upon tense and different truth-value commitments. Some verbs (such as "intend", "prefer", "want", "choose", "desire") are most naturally followed by an infinitive, with or without an accusative, and model their construction on that of reported commands. Others (such as "is glad", "hopes", "regrets") are most naturally followed by a *that*-clause and model their construction on that of reported statements. Others again (such as one use of "wish") are followed by *that*-clauses with subjunctives which model their construction on that of certain *if*-clauses.

If we turn from the reports of affective attitudes to the verbal expression of them we find the same alarming variety. There are, for example, requests, wishes, announcements of intention, and commands issued in first-, second-, and third-person forms. Moreover, some affective attitudes (such as hope, regret) have no verbal expression except in the form of a report. The hope that John will come, for instance, can be expressed verbally neither by the statement "John will come" (for this is compatible with regret that John will come) nor by the wish "If only John would come!" (for this is compatible with despair of John's coming). It can be expressed only by the quasi-report "I hope that John will come".[1] This last circumstance, however, neither simplifies nor complicates our problem; for it is clearly a contingent matter that we do not have special inflections of verbs, as we have special tones of voice, to express hopes and regrets as well as wishes. We might construct sperative and dolitive moods to match the optative.

Can we bring some order into this confusion? Is there some radical difference, of logical importance, between, say, those verbs which use the construction of indirect command and those which use the construction of indirect statement? Or could we devise some artificial construction which would serve the purposes now served by this battery of varied usages?

I believe that we could. The proliferation of different constructions after affective verbs in English can hardly be of logical importance, since no two languages seem to agree on the analogies which they present between reports of different kinds. In Latin, for instance, "volo" uses the construction of indirect speech, while "want" in English uses that of indirect command. I propose, therefore, to introduce an artificial word "to volit" to report quite generally the taking up of an attitude of approval to a state of affairs, no matter whether that state of affairs is actual or possible, past, present or future, likely or unlikely, actualizable by the agent himself or not so actualizable. I shall use "Volition", with a capital letter, as a verbal noun formed from this verb.

The Volition that p will be something which is common to hoping that p, wanting it to be the case

---

[1] It is these quasi-reports which Wittgenstein calls "*Aeusserungen*".

that p, wishing it were the case that p, being glad that p, intending to bring it about that p, regretting that not-p, being ashamed that not-p, fearing that not-p; and which is absent from merely judging that p, believing that p, knowing that p, being certain that p, expecting that p, and not caring a damn whether p. "A volits that p" is therefore equivalent to "*Either* A hopes that p *or* A wants it to be the case that p *or* A regrets that not-p . . .*"; and it could be defined along these lines, had we the patience to fill up the dots.[1]

The theory of desire put forward in the previous chapter may now be more accurately and more generally stated as a theory of Volition. On this theory, A volits that ϕab if and only if A's Idea of a stands in the relation $W(\phi)$ to A's Idea of b.

But now how are we to interpret "W"? Above, an interpretation was sketched in terms of a relation V(punish) which held between expressions occurring in an utterance "God punish England". This utterance might be described as a wish, a prayer, or a command; it was chosen precisely because capable of various descriptions. We may, I think, regard the difference between request and command, and between command and wish, as logically unimportant. Everything which we now do by means of commands and requests addressed to a person could be done by means of wishes mentioning that person. This is, in fact, the procedure in polite Italian. But the form of a wish

[1] I believe that "volit" and "Volition" so defined correspond fairly accurately to the uses of "velle" and "volitio" in medieval philosophical Latin. It will, I hope, be clear that a Volition has nothing in common with Hume's volitions, the mythical nature of which has been well shown by Ryle (*The Concept of Mind*, 62–69).

seems appropriate to report the content of a Volition only in those cases where the carrying out of the Volition depends on some person or factor other than the subject of the Volition. When a wisher is in a position to carry out his own desires, it would seem more natural, in using the "said-in-his heart" construction, to report the Volition by means of a quoted expression of intention than by a quoted command. The desire to go to Innisfree, for instance, might be reported thus: "He said in his heart "I will arise and go now, and go to Innisfree"."

The expression "God punish England" which was used to sketch the interpretation of the relation W(punish) can by no stretch of the imagination be regarded as an expression of intention. But Volition, as now defined, includes intention: a report of a Volition, therefore, may report a mental utterance whose natural form would be that of an expression of intention. By what right, therefore, do I apply to reports of intention an analysis by analogy which commands and wishes? Can an intention be regarded as a command to oneself, or a wish about oneself?

There is, in fact, an important logical feature common to commands, wishes, and expressions of intention, which distinguishes them from statements. If a man sincerely utters a statement which fails to accord with the facts, then he is mistaken; if he utters a command, a wish, or an expression of intention, then he is not mistaken merely because the facts do not accord with his utterance.[1]

[1] This point is well made by Miss Anscombe:

There is a difference between the types of ground on which we call an order, and an estimate of the future, sound. The reasons justifying

But there is another point to set against this. An expression of intention, whether cast in the form "I intend to ϕ" or in the simpler form "I will ϕ" may be a lie. On the other hand, it seems, a command cannot be a lie, nor can a wish. Of course, one can deceive by commanding or wishing; but one can deceive by coughing or snoring or hiding behind an arras; but neither a cough nor a snore nor a stance behind an arras is a lie. Does not this show a major distinction between commands and wishes on the one hand, and expressions of intention on the other?

---

an order are not ones suggesting what is probable or likely to happen but, e.g., ones suggesting what it would be good to make happen with a view to an objective, or with a view to a sound objective. In this regard, commands and expressions of intention are similar. ...

Let us consider a man going round a town with a shopping list in his hand. Now it is clear that the relation of this list to the things he actually buys is one and the same whether his wife gave him the list or it is his own list; and that there is a different relation when a list is made by a detective following him about. If he made the list himself, it was an expression of intention; if his wife gave it to him, it has the role of an order. What then is the identical relation to what happens, in the order and the intention, which is not shared by the record? It is precisely this: if the list and the things that the man actually buys do not agree, and if this and this alone constitutes a *mistake*, then the mistake is not in the list but in the man's performance; whereas if the detective's record and what the man actually buys do not agree, then the mistake is in the record (*Intention*, 4, 56).

Because of this last point Miss Anscombe seems to me to have gone wrong when, following Russell (*Logic and Knowledge*, 228) she says "There is no reason other than a dispensable usage why we should not call commands true and false according as they were obeyed or disobeyed". For if a man, without lying, says something false, then he makes a mistake; but a man who gives a command which is not obeyed, does not therefore make a mistake. I shall indeed argue below that it is possible to be untruthful in giving a command; but a command is untruthful when it is not meant, not when it is not *obeyed*.

P 217

A lie is having one thing in the mouth, and another in the heart: if a man says that p, and says-in-his-heart that not-p, then he lies. Now on our theory, to have the intention (to bring it about) that p, is to say-in-one's-heart "Let it be the case that p". We might therefore think to account for a lie told in the words "I intend to pay you back tomorrow" by saying that it was a statement tantamount to "I have said-in-my-heart "let me pay him back tomorrow" " which is false if I have said-in-my-heart no such thing.

This account is appropriate when "I intend to do such-and-such" is a genuine report of a state of mind, and not the *Aeusserung* of an intention. But where the words uttered are such an *Aeusserung*, as in "I will do such-and-such", then this account will not do. The difficulty, then, comes to this: on the view put forward, "I will do such-and-such" is tantamount to "let me do such-and-such"; but how can this be, since the first expression may be a lie, and the second cannot?

To answer this, we must first remind ourselves that saying to oneself in imagination "let me do such-and-such" is neither a necessary nor a sufficient condition of saying-in-one's-heart "let me do such-and-such"; just as saying to oneself in imagination "I will do such-and-such" is neither a necessary nor a sufficient condition of intending to do such-and-such. Now when such words *are* said, either aloud or to oneself, what is the further condition necessary for them to be a genuine expression of intention, a saying-in-the-heart as well as a saying with the lips or in the head? It is this: that the words should be *meant*.

Wittgenstein writes:

SKETCH OF A THEORY OF VOLITION

When longing makes me cry "Oh, if only he would come!"
the feeling gives the words 'meaning'. But does it give the
individual words their meanings?

But here one could also say that the feeling gave the
words *truth*. And from this you can see how the concepts
merge here (*Philosophical Investigations*, I, 544).

The concept of *meaning an utterance* which Wittgenste in
here distinguishes from the concept of *the meaning of
an utterance* has application to statements as well as
to wishes. "When he said that the man in the moon
would gobble you up, he didn't mean it." "It was only
a joke" and "It was just a story" are two common ways
of denying that a statement was *meant*, that is, meant
to be taken seriously.

Now this notion of *meaning* plays different parts in
connection with statements and in connection with
commands. For a statement to be either truthful or
untruthful, it must be meant; and a truthful statement differs from an untruthful one in being *believed*
by the utterer. But a command or a wish is sincere if it
is *meant* by the utterer, and insincere if it is not. We
can therefore distinguish between statements on the
one hand, and commands and wishes on the other,
by saying that for the former the criterion of sincerity
is belief, and for the latter the criterion of sincerity is
meaning them.

The expression of an intention in the form of a
statement about the future is condemned as a lie not
on the grounds merely that it is not fulfilled (not even
if the non-fulfilment is voluntary), nor yet merely
because the utterer does not expect it to be fulfilled;
but only on the grounds that the expression of the
intention is not *meant*. In this respect, therefore,

expressions of intention turn out after all to be like commands and wishes and unlike statements.

There is no reason, therefore, why we should not, as our theory demands, regard an expression of intention as a command uttered to oneself or a wish about oneself. The insincere expression of intention may be regarded as giving oneself an order, in the presence of one's listener, which one does not mean oneself to obey. It is as if a superior, having received a complaint against a subordinate, should summon the subordinate and tell him in the complainer's presence "Put this matter right", though both superior and subordinate know that the command is not meant seriously and is issued merely to satisfy the complainer.

Compared with the distinction between the assessing of sincerity by reference to belief and by reference to meaning, the question whether to call a particular insincere utterance "a lie" is comparatively trivial. We naturally call an insincere expression of intention a lie simply because it has the grammatical form of a statement. But if a man does not wish me to come, are we to say that he lies if he says "I wish you would come!" but not if he says "If only you would come"? If a lie is distinguished from other forms of deceit by being the deceitful abuse *of a significant symbol*, then an insincere wish is a lie no less than an insincere statement. And both statements and commands differ from coughs and snores; for though one can deceive by coughs and snores, and emit feigned coughs and snores, there are no such things as insincere coughs or insincere snores.

Despite, therefore, the varied constructions which follow affective verbs, it seems that the one distinction of logical importance is between two modes of speech which we may call the indicative and the optative. In the first mode, the facts, or what happens, sets the standard by which the utterance is judged and found true or false; in the second mode, the utterance sets the standard by which the facts, or what happens, is judged and found good or bad. *Verum et falsum in mente, bonum et malum in rebus.* That is to say, whether a statement or a belief is true or false depends on what the facts are; the facts are the standard by which statements and beliefs are judged. On the other hand, whether an agent makes a mistake in what he does depends on what his intentions are; whether a subject's actions are obedient or disobedient depends on what his master's commands were; whether a citizen acts legally or illegally depends on what the laws are; whether a particular state of affairs is good or bad depends on what somebody wants.[1] In all these cases, a Volition is the standard by which what happens is judged.[2]

[1] There is an important difference, not often noticed, between describing a state of affairs as good, and describing a thing as good. The criteria for the goodness of a thing depends on the nature of the thing in question: an earthworm who does well the things that earthworms do is a good earthworm, no matter whether anybody wants an earthworm or not. The criteria for the goodness of a state of affairs depend on what people want: good weather is not weather which is good of its kind, or which does well the things which weather does, but weather which enables you to do well whatever it is you want to do.

[2] The three traditional kinds of utterance are statement, command, and question. But questions need not be regarded as a third fundamental class of utterances, since they may be looked at as a form of command. Thus "has the post come?" is equivalent to "say "the post has come" or "the post has not come" according as the post has come or not come". "What is the capital of England" can be asked, as it is on some examination papers, in the form "Fill in the blank in the sentence-frame "... is the capital of England".

This, too, then, is a feature which our theory must preserve, however, it is modified: it must preserve a radical distinction, as well as a parallel, between Volition and judgement.

The next objection to our theory comes from the opposite quarter. Does not the theory make Volition seem *too unlike* judgement? Let us ask: what is the relation between our two operators "Z" and "W"? All that they have in common is that they are both non-extensional operators, that they both share the polyadicity of their base, and that the relations formed by them hold between the same class of entities, namely Ideas. There is no more in common between, say, the relation Z(defeat) and the relation W(defeat) than there is between the relation *louder than* and the relation *longer than*. Is this correct? And if not, is it the best we can do?

Consider the following passage of Wittgenstein's *Philosophical Investigations:*

Imagine a picture representing a boxer in a particular stance. Now, this picture can be used to tell someone how he should stand, should hold himself; or how he should not hold himself; or how a particular man did stand in such-and-such a place. One might (using the language of chemistry) call this picture a sentence-radical.[1]

We may apply this illustration to Geach's theory of judgement, and our theory of Volition. Using the picture to tell someone how to stand is like command-

[1] The passage occurs in a footnote to p. 11, where Wittgenstein is discussing Frege's assertion sign.

ing; using the picture to tell someone how a particular man stands is like asserting. The judgement "such and such a boxer stands so" will, on Geach's theory, consist of the predicate "Z(stand so)" 's holding of the judger's Idea of *boxer*.[1]

Now it is clear that in the analogy, the pictured boxer corresponds to the judger's Idea of boxer; and it seems natural to say that what corresponds to the predicate "Z(stand so)"'s holding is (the pictured boxer's) *being pictured as standing so*. But this is wrong, because the picture is the same whether it is used to make an assertion or a command; and so the pictured boxer is pictured in the same way whether the predicate holding of the corresponding Idea is "Z(stand so)" or "W(stand so)". The disposition of the elements of the picture is common both to the assertion and the command made by its means; and what makes the difference between assertion and command cannot be part of the picture itself.

Professor Stenius, following a suggestion of R. M. Hare's, has recently given us a developed exposition of the concept of a 'sentence-radical'. He remarks that the sentences "You live here now" and "Live here now!" correspond to one another in this way: that what is the case if the first is true is also the case if the second is obeyed. What is in common to the two sentences is what Hare calls "the phrastic" of the

---

[1] To make a reference to a particular boxer, the judgement would have to stand in relation to a sensory context, and various other conditions would have to hold (*Mental Acts*, 61–74).

It is to be noted that Geach does not himself apply his theory to judgements involving one-place predicates; but it must be possible so to do, if the theory is to fulfil the conditions Geach himself lays down (*Ibid.*, 49).

sentence (*The Language of Morals*, 11f.) and what Wittgenstein called the "sentence-radical". Both sentences, Stenius says, describe the same state of affairs, but present it in a different mood. We must therefore distinguish in any sentence between the sentence-radical which shows the state of affairs (real or imagined) that the sentence describes, and a modal component, which indicates what function the presentation of this state of affairs has in communication. "The state of affairs presented," Stenius writes, "is the *descriptive content* of the sentence, the function is a semantical component which may be called its semantical *mood*. The sentence-radical thus indicates the descriptive content; the functional, or, as it may also be called, *modal* component, indicates the mood. The modal component need not appear as a separate sign in the sentence; but it must be a characteristic that can in some way be noticed in the sentence when it is produced as a "move in the language-game" ".[1]

Stenius goes on to discuss various modal operators which form sentences out of sentence-radicals, notably the deontic operators of von Wright.[2] He introduces also a modal operator "I" as a sign of the indicative

[1] *Wittgenstein's Tractatus*, 161. Stenius presents his distinction between descriptive content and mood in the course of a discussion of the picture theory of meaning put forward in the *Tractatus*; but the distinction retains its use whether or not the relation between a sentence-radical and the state of affairs it describes is most helpfully explained as one of picturing.

[2] Note that this is a different sense of "operator" from that used, e.g., by Wittgenstein in the *Tractatus* (5.251, etc.), For Wittgenstein, it is a defining property of an operator that the result of an operation can be its own base; Stenius' operators do not possess this property, and therefore are operators only in the sense in which predicates are operators which form sentence-radicals out of names.

mood: a sentence in the indicative is to be rendered "Ip", where "p" takes the place, not of a sentence, but of a sentence-radical. He observes that for the operator "I", unlike the other modal operators he considers (such as "It is obligatory that . . .", "It is necessary that . . ."), the following rule holds: "NIp" is equivalent to "INp".

After his opening remarks, Stenius rather oddly drops the subject of imperatives; he does not discuss any operator which would form a command out of a sentence-radical. Let us introduce such an operator "T"; "Tp" will have the force of "Let it be the case that p". We may notice that for this operator a rule holds analogous to that for "I"; that is to say, the command "Let it not be the case that p" is equivalent to the command "Let it be the case that not-p" just as "NIp" is equivalent to "INp".

Stenius uses *that*-clauses for sentence-radicals, such as "that you live here now". Compared with Hare's use of verbal nouns of the type "your living here now", Stenius' method has the disadvantage that the form of the verb in the *that*-clause may carry with it an irrelevant suggestion of the indicative mood. But it has the more important advantage that it makes clear that a sentence-radical is itself necessarily complex, made up of function and argument, and describing a state of affairs and not a thing. The relation between subject and predicate is already there in the sentence-radical; it is not made by assertion, commanding, querying or any other modal operation upon it.

The plea for a distinction between predication and assertion goes back, in recent times, to Frege and

Brentano.[1] Long before this, the distinction was made by Aquinas, and explicitly applied to theory of judgement. In his commentary on the *De Interpretatione* Aquinas discusses Aristotle's dictum that truth and falsehood belong to combination and division. He remarks that by "division" Aristotle frequently means a negative judgement, and raises the difficulty: are not subject and predicate combined in a negative proposition no less than in an affirmative one? He writes:

If we consider what takes place in the mind by itself then there is always combination where there is truth and falsehood; for the mind cannot produce anything true or false unless it combines one simple concept with another. But if the relation to reality is taken into account, then the mind's operation is called sometimes "combination" and sometimes "division"; "combination" where the mind so places one concept beside another as to represent the combination or identity of the things *of* which they are the concepts; "division" where it so places one concept beside another as to represent that the corresponding realities are distinct. We talk in the same way of sentences too: an affirmative sentence is called "a combination" because it signifies that there is a conjunction in reality; a negative sentence is called "a division" because it signifies that the realities are separate.[2]

---

[1] Frege: *Philosophical Writings*, 34; Brentano: *Psychologie vom Empirischen Standpunkt*, II, 7, 5ff. Brentano says: "Die Zusammensetzung aus Subjekt and Prädikat ist keineswegs etwas, was der Natur des Urteils wesentlich ist, und die Unterscheidung der beiden Bestandteile hangt vielmehr nun mit einer gemeinüblichen Form des sprachlichen Ausdruckes zusammen" (Ed. Kraus, I, 201).

[2] *Si consideremus ea quae sunt circa intellectum secundum se, semper est compositio, ubi est veritas et falsitas; quae nunquam invenitur in intellectu, nisi per hoc quod intellectus comparat unum simplicem conceptum alteri. Sed si referatur ad rem, quandoque dicitur compositio,*

The "combination" that is present in any judgement corresponds to the complexity which is essential to the sentence-radical; we might call the complex formed by this composition a 'thought-radical', using "thought" to stand indifferently for a judgement, a wish, or an intention, as Stenius uses "sentence" to stand indifferently for a statement, a command, or a question. The *compositio* which is a special relation to reality in which the mind sets its 'thought-radical' when it makes an affirmative judgement corresponds to the modal operator which makes the sentence-radical into a statement. Aquinas is here in effect considering assertion and denial as two independent modal operations upon essentially positive sentence-radicals. Whether this is a necessary, or a possible, way of explaining the matter is open to discussion; our present point is merely that Aquinas distinguished between assertion and predication. He recognized also that there were other forms of speech besides affirmative and negative statements which shared the subject-predicate complexity of statements, yet which were neither true nor false. He lists four such modes: deprecative, imperative, interrogative, and vocative.[1]

[1] By "the vocative mood" Aquinas means the mood of an exclamation, such as "you silly fool!", not the use of a man's name to call him. ("*Non est vocativa oratio nisi plura coniungantur: ut cum dico o*

quandoque dicitur divisio. Compositio quidem, quando intellectus comparat unum conceptum alteri, quasi apprehendens coniunctionem aut identitatem rerum, quarum sunt conceptiones; divisio autem, quando sic comparat unum conceptum alteri, ut apprehendat res esse diversas. Et per hunc etiam modum in vocibus affirmatio dicitur compositio, in quantum coniunctionem ex parte rei significat; negatio vero dicitur divisio in quantum significat rerum separationem (In I Periherm. I, 3 ed. Spiazzi, 26). For a good commentary on this and parallel texts see P. Hoenen, S.J., La Théorie du Jugement d'après St Thomas d'Aquin, 11–17.

Geach himself has repeatedly drawn attention to the distinction between predication and assertion. Recently, for example, he has written:

In order that the use of a sentence in which "P" is predicated of a thing may count as an act of *calling* the thing "P", the sentence must be used assertively; and this is something quite distinct from predication, for, as we have remarked, "P" may still be predicated of the thing even in a sentence used nonassertively as a clause within another sentence. Hence calling a thing "P" has to be explained in terms of predicating "P" of the thing, not the other way round.[1]

In view of this, it is surprising that Geach, in his theory of judgement, lumps together predication and assertion; for that is what he does. In effect, he has given us, not a theory of judgement, but the sketch of a theory of thought-radicals. The common element between judgement and Volition which we felt had not been made clear was precisely the element corresponding to predication. *Punishing England* is predicated of God no less in "God punish England!" than in "God punishes England"; our account of

[1] *"Ascriptivism,"* in *The Philosophical Review*, April 1960, 223. Geach is here thinking of the occurrence of sentences in *if*-clauses and the like. Such an occurrence is, of course, quite different from the 'occurrence' of a sentence-radical in a sentence. In "if *p* then *q*" the variables take the place, not of sentence-radicals, but of something which on the face of it itself has a mood. "If the pubs are open, be sure to have a drink" is quite different from "If the pubs are open, you are sure to be having a drink". But the distinction between predication and assertion is manifest in the distinction between statements and commands no less than in the distinction between assertive and nonassertive uses of sentences.

bone Petre", *Op. cit.* ed. Spiazzi, 85). Aristotle noted the existence of non-indicative moods: he thought they were best left to the poets (*De Interpretatione*, 17 a 5).

saying-in-one's-heart each of these things failed to make this clear as it should have done. There is *some* relation which holds between a man's Idea of *God* and his Idea of *England* no matter whether he judges that God punishes England or he wants God to punish England. Any theory of judgement or volition should make this common element clear.

To do so, I shall first extend the use of the verb "to predicate" to cover the use of other than monadic predicates. We are accustomed to saying that when I assert that ϕa, one of the things I do is to predicate ϕing of a. Let us say also that if a man asserts that ϕab, then one of the things he does is to predicate ϕing of a to b; and if he asserts that ϕba, then one of the things he does is to predicate ϕing of b to a. Since we have considered judging that p as mentally stating that p, and Voliting that p as mentally wishing that p; and since we have called the element common to stating and wishing "predicating"; let us call the element common to judging and Voliting "mentally predicating". The use of this terminology in no way commits us to the view that there is some mental act which consists merely in, say, placing two Ideas in relation to each other without thereby either making a judgement or producing a Volition. Such a procedure would not be a mental act any more than a sentence-radical is a move in any language-game; and it may be no more capable of separate performance than a chemical radical is capable of existence in isolation. It is, however, the case that we have a mode of reporting mental acts, as we have of reporting speech, which does not commit us to any statement about the mood of the speech or the corresponding feature of the mental act. We may say "He was thinking of asking the Archbishop to open the bazaar", as we may say "He was talking of asking the Archbishop to open the bazaar". We may do so either when we mean that he had, or expressed, the intention of asking the Archbishop to open the bazaar; or that he had, or expressed, the thought how foolish it was to ask the Archbishop to open the bazaar; or merely that he recalled, in thought or speech, that distant but never-to-be-forgotten day on which he asked, etc.

We are now in a position to revise Geach's theory of judgement and our own of Volition. Let us scrap the two operators "Z" and "W" and substitute for them a single operator "P", of the same logical type (non-extensional operator forming predicates out of predicates without altering polyadicity). Let us then say that when James *either* judges *or* Volits that ϕab (that is to say, when he mentally predicates ϕing of a to b), then his Idea of a stands in the relation $P(\phi)$ to his Idea of b. We have thus substituted for our previous theories of judgement and Volition a theory of mental predication which will do part of the work of, and preserve the advantages of, both theories.

How are we now to complete the theory by expressing the difference between judgement and Volition, which corresponds to the difference between the operators "I" and "T"? "I" and "T" are symbols which are added to symbols for states of affairs in order to make them into commands or statements. What we want is a symbol *for* the mental operation which corresponds to the placing of "I" or "T" in front of a sentence-radical, or (in ordinary language) to giving the appropriate modal inflection to the verb. What kind of symbol do we want? We cannot use two further operators on predicates; for these would merely give us, e.g., two further relations between Ideas; whereas we want to represent a mental operation on the complex which is formed by the Ideas standing in a certain relation to each other.

Let us write, as a symbol for the complex which is formed by a in the relation ϕ to b, "$[\phi ab]$".[1] The complex which is formed by a mental predication of A of ϕing of a to b will then be symbolized by "$[P\phi a'b']$". We must also introduce two predicates: one which must hold of such a complex if it is to be an act of judgement, and the other which must hold of it if it is to be an act of Volition. Let "J" be an abbreviation for the first predicate, and "H" for the second. Then we have:[2]

A judges that ϕab if and only if $I(J[P\phi a'b'])$

A volits that ϕab if and only if $I(H[P\phi a'b'])$

If we can now offer an interpretation of the predicates "J" and "H" we shall have completed our theory of judgement and Volition. To define them would be a task of Gordian complication; but perhaps we can suggest the main outlines of them in one example.

Suppose that the two reports which we wish to analyse are "James judges that Communism will supplant Capitalism" and "James wishes Communism to supplant Capitalism". As the first step in our analy-

---

[1] For the square-bracket notation compare, for example, Wittgenstein *Notebooks* 1914–16, 119.

[2] "I" as before as the mark of the indicative mood. Stenius gives a bracketing convention whereby the operator "I" can almost always be omitted (*Op. cit.*, 163). Henceforth, as in earlier chapters, I shall follow this convention, taking "p" as an assertion and signifying the sentence-radical belonging to it by "(p)".

sis, we replace these reports by "James says in his heart "Communism will supplant Capitalism" " and "James says in his heart "May Communism supplant Capitalism" " respectively. If either of these reports is true, James's mental utterance of "Communism" stands in the relation P(supplant) to his mental utterance of "Capitalism". These two mental utterances stand in this relation to each other if and only if each of them forms part of a mental utterance of an expression, any physical occurrence of which consists of utterances by one and the same person of a series of expressions which (a) taken together forms part of no other expression (b) contains the expressions "Communism", "supplant" and "Capitalism" in that order and (c) contains no other expressions other than symbols indicating the mood and tense of the expression as a whole.

We may now interpret, for this example, the predicates "J" and "H". The predicate "J" holds of the complex which consists of James's mental utterance of "Communism" standing in the relation P(supplant) to James's mental utterance of "Capitalism" if and only if the mood-indicating symbol referred to in the definition of "P(supplant)" is the expression "will" occurring between the expressions "Communism" and "supplant". The predicate "H" holds of the complex if and only if the mood-indicating symbol is the word "may" occurring before the expression "Communism".

To allow for the very large number of ways in which mood may be expressed in English, as well as the different types of predicate which may occur in both statements and command, not to mention the possibilities of filling out sentences with greater detail, any generalized definition of the predicates "J" and "H" or of the operator "P" would be impossibly long. But the difficulties which remain in this part of our analysis are, if I am not mistaken, difficulties of complication and not of principle.

Our theory, however, is not yet complete. We have constructed a theory of Volition which is completely parallel to a theory of judgement and which explains Volition ultimately in terms of Ideas, or exercises of concepts. But in fact volition is not completely parallel to judgement, and it cannot be explained by reference to Ideas without reference to action. To put it crudely: what a man *does* enters into what he wills in a way in which it does not enter into what he believes; a complete theory of volition must therefore mention actions as well as thoughts.

In chapter 4 of *Mental Acts* Geach makes the point, against Ryle, that there is no behaviour characteristic of a given belief, other than putting it into words. Unless we know the needs or wants of an agent, we cannot tell what counts as "acting as if you held such and such a belief". We can indeed attribute beliefs to animals, though they cannot put them into words; but this is because we know their needs and can attribute wants to them on the basis of their behaviour. We can also speak of the behaviour characteristic of particular emotions; but this is because any report of an emotion ascribes *both* a belief *and* a want to a subject. But for believing divorced from wanting there is no characteristic manifestation in non-verbal behaviour. It is for this reason that it is legitimate to analyse judgement in terms of a relation holding only between Ideas.

Now there *are* volitions which, like beliefs, have no natural non-verbal expression. Among such volitions are idle wishes about states of affairs over which one has no control (such as the wish that the universe might be annihilated, or that the Cavaliers had won the Civil War), regrets about one's own past actions which are beyond mending, and in general volitions about states of affairs which one is powerless to bring about. For some people, the only possible manifestation of the wish to have their tie tied is the request to their wife to tie it. For such cases, our account of Volition suffices. Above, Volition was indeed defined as the element common to all volitions, even the most tenuous and ineffective volitions: it was therefore appropriate to explain it in terms of Ideas, without reference to deeds. But if we are to give an account of more full-blooded volitions, and in particular of voluntary activity which is the paradigm of volition, we must take account of something more than Volition.

Desire manifests itself not only in the utterance of commands and wishes, but also in behaviour; one obvious manifestation of *wanting* X is *trying to get* X, and the will that *p* shows itself in efforts to bring it about that *p*. Aquinas lists five ways in which volition is manifested: *operatio, permissio, praeceptum, consilium* and *prohibitio* (*Summa Theologica*, I, 19, 12). Disregarding his distinction between command and suasion, we are left with four manifestations of volition, two behavioural and two linguistic. The will that *p* may be manifested by bringing it about that *p*,

234

by not bringing it about that not-p, by commanding that p, and by forbidding that not-p. Our analysis of Volition concerned only the third, though it can be easily adapted to fit the fourth. We must now turn to the first two.

It might be thought that volition was, after all, quite parallel to belief. For if we must know what a man wants in order to take his behaviour as evidence of a belief, must we not also know what he believes in order to infer from his behaviour what he wants? Behaviour may be quite inappropriate to bring about a desired result; but as long as the agent *believes* it to be appropriate, it may manifest his desire for the result. To prove that there is no natural non-verbal manifestation of a belief, Geach gives the example of Dr Johnson standing bareheaded in Uttoxeter market: we can infer from h is behaviour that he expects rain only if we know thathe wants to get wet in order to do penance. Can we not equally say that we must know that he expects rain in order to recognize his behaviour as a sign of the desire to do penance? If this example is typical, then we must say that there is no behaviour characteristic of either a belief or a volition, but only behaviour characteristic of some combination of the two. But this is not so. The example of Dr Johnson is not typical (since wanting to do penance involves wanting to do something which one does not want to do, e.g. to get wet) and the objection which I have used it to make does not stand. What a man does and what a man says he wants may conflict; and what he does may be a better guide to what he wants than what he says he wants, even if he is perfectly sincere. Now it was a sufficient, though not a necessary, criterion for a man's having the Volition that p that he should sincerely say that he wanted that p. It follows that his having the Volition that p is not always a sufficient condition for his having the volition that p.

The most notorious cases in which what a man sincerely says conflicts with what he does are the cases which lead psychoanalysts to speak of 'unconscious desires'. There are simpler cases: we all make resolutions and fail to keep them; we wish we were better men but our actions show that we don't really want to be. But in the standard case of voluntary activity, what a man does accords with his Volition, that is, with what he can sincerely say he wants. Now we saw earlier in Chapter 8 that the primary form of description of a piece of voluntary behaviour takes the form of a performance verb. We saw also that any performance verb can be replaced by an expression of the form "bringing it about that p" where "(p)" describes the state of affairs which is the result of the process. In the normal case of voluntary action, therefore, a man both volits that p and is bringing it about that p. Thus, when a man is (voluntarily) washing his face, he both volits that his face be clean, and is bringing it about that his face is clean. This is the kernel of my theory of the will: it remains to complete it.

The theory is not complete as it stands; for it may be the case that a man both volits that p, and is bringing it about that p, and yet his action in bringing it about that p may not be voluntary, or not fully voluntary. A bather may stand on the bank of a river, intending shortly to dive in, and while he stands there be pushed in by a friend; in such a case he volits to be in the water, and his own motion in falling brings it about that he is in the water;[1] yet his falling is not voluntary. Still, in such a case we might say that it is at least partly voluntary, if he could have stopped himself falling by clutching at a tree: his behaviour will then be a manifestation of desire of Aquinas' second type: not bringing it about that not-*p*, *letting himself* fall in (*permissio*).

In view of this, we must add a further qualification; so that our account now runs: Where ϕing is bringing it about that *p*, then A ϕs voluntarily only if A volits that *p*, and A brings it about that *p*, *and it is in A's power not to bring it about that* p.

Even with this qualification, our account is not complete. Consider the following case: a man, having written a suicide note, electrocutes himself on a faulty switch while entering the kitchen to put his head in the oven. Such a man does not commit suicide, i.e. does not kill himself voluntarily, but dies by accident. Yet he had the Volition to be dead, by touching the switch he brought it about that he was dead, and it was in his power not to kill himself, for he did not have to touch the switch. In this case, the man did not *know* that by touching the switch he would bring about his own death. So we must add knowledge to our conditions for voluntary action and say that for A

[1] It is necessary to stress that the sense of "bringing it about that . . ." here, and in Chapter 8 above, is not equivalent to "voluntarily bringing it about that . . .". Anything which is the result of the movements of a man's body, voluntary or involuntary, is in this sense "brought about" by him; as a stove may bring it about that a kettle is hot, without there being any question here of volition on the part of the stove.

voluntarily to bring it about that p, he must know that he is bringing it about that p.

Yet a man may want an enemy of his to be dead, and knowingly cause his death when it was in his power not to do so, and yet not be a murderer; if, for example, he is a soldier who is ordered in wartime to blow up a bridge on which his personal enemy is standing guard; or if he leaves him to burn in a blazing building because he has only time to rescue one victim, and rescues his own wife instead. In such cases, though the man wants his enemy to die, yet he does not cause him to die *because* he wants him to die.

We must say, then, that for a man's action to be fully voluntary, it must, besides fulfilling the conditions already laid down, stand in a special relation to his Volition. This relation is expressed by the use of the word "because" in the sentence which ended the last paragraph; but *what* it is I am unable at present to say. It is clearly not sufficient, in general, that the agent should *say* that it is not because he wants to that he is doing such-and-such; there must be some test of his sincerity in saying this. The ways in which we do test a man's sincerity when he says this sort of thing are very complicated indeed; which explains why it should be so difficult to give an account of the relation between Volition and action.[1]

Aquinas called the relation "being commanded by the will": fully voluntary action was *actus imperatus a voluntate*. This is only a metaphor; but I think that it is the right metaphor. The relation between Volition and action has throughout our account been explained by analogy with the relation between a

[1] Cf. Miss Anscombe, *Intention*, 42–44.

command and its fulfilment. And just as there are cases where it is very difficult to decide whether a man does something *because* he wants to, so it is sometimes very difficult to decide whether a man does something *because* he has been commanded to. Our methods of deciding the latter question are our only clue to deciding the former.[1]

Cf. Wittgenstein *Philosophical Investigations*, 1, 487–490.

BIBLIOGRAPHY

ALBERTUS, MAGNUS, *Summa de Bono*

ANSCOMBE, G. E. M., *Intention*, Oxford, 1957

— *An Introduction to Wittgenstein's Tractatus*, London, 1959

AQUINAS, THOMAS, *Summa Theologica*

— *In II Libros Perihermeneias Aristotelis Expositio*

ARISTOTLE, *Metaphysics*

— *Nicomachean Ethics*

— *De Anima*

— *Rhetoric*

BLATZ, W., "The cardiac, respiratory and electrical phenomena involved in the emotion of fear". *J. Exper. Psychol*, 1925

BRENTANO, F., *Psychologie vom Empirischen Standpunkt* (ed. Kraus), Hamburg, 1955

CANNON, W. B., *Bodily Changes in Pain, Hunger, Fear and Rage*, Boston, 1929

CHISHOLM, R. M., *Perceiving: A Philosophical Study*, Cornell, 1957

DESCARTES, R., *Les Passions de l'Ame*

— *Philosophical Writings: a Selection Translated and Edited by Elizabeth Anscombe & Peter Thomas Geach*, London, 1952

DEUTSCH, J. A., *The Structural Basis of Behaviour*, Cambridge, 1960

DUNBAR, F., *Emotions and Bodily Changes*, Columbia, 1954

FLUGEL, C., *Studies in Feeling and Desire*, London, 1955

FREGE, G., *Translations from the Philosophical Writings of Gottlob Frege*, by P. Geach and M. Black, Oxford, 1952

FREUD, S., *Beyond the Pleasure Principle* (English Collected Works, vol. XVIII), London, 1953

GEACH, P. T., *Mental Acts*, London, 1957

GOSLING, J. C. B., "False pleasures in the Philebus", *Phronesis* 4, 1959

HACKFORTH, C., *Plato's Examination of Pleasure*, Cambridge, 1945

HARE, R. M., *The Language of Morals*, Oxford, 1952

HEBB, D. O., *A Textbook of Psychology*, London and N.Y., 1955

HILLMAN, J., *Emotion*, London, 1960

HOENEN, P., *La Théorie du judgement d'après St Thomas d'Aquin*, Rome, 1946

HUME, D., *A Treatise of Human Nature*

— *An Enquiry concerning Human Understanding*

HUSSERL, E., *Ideen zu einer reinen Phänomenologie und phänomenologischen Philosophie*, I, Haag 1950

JAMES, W., *Principles of Psychology* (Dover edn.) London, and N.Y., 1950

LOCKE, J., *An Essay concerning Human Understanding*

NOWELL-SMITH, P., *Ethics*, London, 1955

PLATO, *Philebus*

PRIOR, A. N., *Formal Logic*, Oxford, 1955

— *Time and Modality*, Oxford, 1958

RUCKMICK, C. A., *The Psychology of Feeling and Emotion*, N.Y. and London, 1936

RUSSELL, B., *The Analysis of Mind*, London, 1921

— *An Inquiry into Meaning and Truth*, London, 1940

— *Logic and Knowledge*, London, 1956

RYLE, G., *The Concept of Mind*, London, 1948

STENIUS, E., *Wittgenstein's Tractatus*, Oxford, 1960

WITTGENSTEIN, L., *Tractatus Logico-Philosophicus*, London, 1922

— *Philosophical Investigations*, Oxford, 1953

— *The Blue and Brown Books*, Oxford, 1958

— *Notebooks* 1914–1916, Oxford, 1960

WOODWORTH, *Experimental Psychology*, London, 1950

INDEX